Unlearned Lessons

Unlearned Lessons

Six Stumbling Blocks
to Our Schools' Success

W. JAMES POPHAM

HARVARD EDUCATION PRESS
CAMBRIDGE, MASSACHUSETTS

Library of Congress Control Number 2008942556
Paperback ISBN 978-1-934742-14-3
Library Edition ISBN 978-1-934742-15-0

Published by Harvard Education Press,
an imprint of the Harvard Education Publishing Group
Harvard Education Press
8 Story Street
Cambridge, MA 02138

Cover Design: Perry Lubin

The typefaces used in this book are Gill Sans and Sabon.

Contents

Preface

I was seventy-seven years old when I started writing this book, so I thought I'd better hurry. Besides, you'd think a pair of lucky sevens would augur well for any book's success.

But longevity qualms and lucky numbers aside, what finally pushed me into beginning the book was a simple case of exasperation. Having been a public school educator for well over a half-century, I finally became fed up with seeing today's educators making precisely the same sorts of mistakes I'd seen educators make, again and again, in earlier years. If there's any truth in the saying, "Those who don't learn from their mistakes are destined to repeat them," why is it that today's educators seem almost compelled to replicate their predecessors' blunders?

I realize that we sometimes find it satisfying to see individuals who, unable to profit from their earlier missteps, continue to make the same mistakes. After all, we surmise, if they aren't smart enough to learn from their errors, then they richly deserve whatever flows their way. Unfortunately, however, when educators make mistakes, they rarely err in isolation, and those who lose out are almost always students. This is why I find it so exasperating when educators repeat their predecessors' mistakes. Repeat mistakes are bad enough; repeat mistakes made by educators are inexcusable.

Mistakes, of course, happen. Educators, like all human beings, will make errors as they carry out their work. A teacher, for instance, may try out a brand-new technique that, despite the teacher's best hopes, flops rather than flies. The new technique was simply ineffective. When such mistakes occur, however, any sensible teacher simply figures out what went wrong, corrects this shortcoming, then teaches differently when next year's students roll in.

I've spent many years teaching and, as a consequence, I've made hundreds of instructional mistakes that required fixing. Accordingly, I definitely don't get upset about any teacher's fumble-and-fix approach to classroom instruction. Instructional mistakes in the classroom are certain to be made—and most of them are readily correctable.

What distresses me, however, are the sorts of mistakes that have a negative impact on a large number of classrooms. The kinds of educational errors I'm referring to are policy decisions—typically rules or regulations made by authorities at the federal, state, and district levels—that have a negative impact on the way many teachers are trying to teach many students. These mistaken policy decisions are the kinds of mistakes I've chosen to write about in this book.

SIX UNLEARNED LESSONS

In the book's first six chapters, I'll describe a half-dozen *unlearned lessons,* that is, six specific mistakes educators persist in making—repeat mistakes that harm students educationally. I've *not* selected these six unlearned lessons because they represent the most significant problems we need to address in education but, rather, because they're serious mistakes I've encountered "up close and personal" during my own career. Putting it differently, I've chosen to deal with these particular mistakes because I'm intimately familiar with all six of them—either having made the mistake myself or having observed, first-hand, others making a particular mistake. I'll be dealing with both *errors of commission* and *errors of omission.* Either of those kinds of mistakes can be costly.

In education, an error of commission occurs when someone's action has an adverse effect on educational quality—for example, if a school board establishes a new test-analysis procedure that is so time-consuming that teachers literally have no time left for instructional planning. Errors of commission are fairly easy to spot, especially once their adverse effects become apparent.

Errors of omission can also have a negative impact on schooling, such as when someone's failure to act or respond has a damaging effect on educational quality—for example, if a school principal refuses to orient new teachers to the school's classroom-management policies and it leads to a flock of serious disciplinary flare-ups in their classrooms.

For each of these six unlearned lessons, I'll first describe the nature of the mistake and its negative impact on schooling. Then I'll toss in a sidebar or two that details a personal run-in with this specific mistake. Finally, before leaving each lesson, I'll close with a recommended way of rectifying this mistake.

I want to reiterate that there are ways to bring about more profound improvement in our schools than by fixing the six problems I'll be addressing. For example, suppose we were able to massively increase the dollars we spend on education so that, as a consequence, we could bump up the salaries of public school teachers by, say, 50 percent—we'd surely be able to recruit a host of talented people into the teaching profession. And if we had more talented teachers, it would certainly improve the caliber of instruction our students receive. I'm not suggesting that there aren't tons of talented teachers currently staffing our schools. Many of today's teachers are of course terrifically skilled, but dramatically higher salaries would entice many capable new people to become teachers, and a continuing influx of such individuals would surely have a positive and long-lasting impact on educational quality.

But what's the likelihood of our seeing enough of an increase in the level of school funding to lead to a strengthened teaching force? I've been hearing people call for higher teacher salaries most of my life—I first heard such pleas way back when I was still a student in high school. Therefore, I've listened to those "more-money" requests off and on for well over sixty years but I've never seen any meaningful action taken in response to them.

Certain profound shortcomings in education are simply so costly to rectify that they're unlikely to be remedied. Other educational problems are so deeply engrained that they'll take a very long time to address successfully. Those sorts of mistakes represent targets too elusive for my taste. I want to tackle a more tangible set of mistakes that can be fixed affordably, realistically, and quickly—like those reflected in the six unlearned lessons, which can be remedied in short order if we tackle them head on.

If the mistakes I'll be discussing were all to be remedied in the next few years, would America's public schools suddenly become pedagogical paradises? Of course not! But I'm convinced that if one or more of the six mistakes were actually fixed, there would be a clear, discernible improvement in our schools—one of our own making that would definitely benefit kids.

This book is not intended to be merely "an interesting read." Oh, of course I'll not be offended if you find it somewhat interesting. But if the book fails to generate the kind of actions intended to remedy one or more of the six mistakes it identifies, then it will surely be a failure. The mistakes to be treated, I assure you, are eminently fixable, and the people reading this book can have a hand in mending them. Clearly, the book was written with a mission in mind. I want to see at least some of the book's six repeat-mistakes remedied. If one or more of these mistake are fixed, then some of our children will receive a better education.

Just a few paragraphs ago, I indicated that most of the mistakes I'll be dealing with in the book were made by "authorities at the federal, state, and district levels." For instance, the mistake-makers might be legislators, appointed officials such as state education commissioners, or the elected members of local or state school boards. Suppose, therefore, that you are not one of these "authorities," but a teacher, a school administrator, a parent of a school-age child, or an everyday citizen. Does this mean that you can't play a role in fixing these mistakes? On the contrary—you can most definitely participate if you decide to do so. Are you personally obliged to take some sort of action? Of course you aren't, but I do hope some readers will take action after finishing the book.

In chapter 7, the book's final chapter, I'll try to entice some readers into tackling one or more of the problems treated in the foregoing six chapters. I hope you'll take a serious look at the suggestions in that chapter, because the longer we allow our schools to suffer from the six unlearned lessons, the more children there are who will get a lower quality education than they deserve.

Now, just before dipping into the first of education's unlearned lessons, I need to get a bit personal. You may wonder what led me to a career in teaching and then in assessment, and how I came to write this book. My college major was in Aristotelian philosophy, and because there was zero demand for Aristotelian philosophers in the mid-fifties job market, I decided to become a high school teacher. Although I taught for two years in a high school in eastern Oregon and loved it, it was clear that my teacher-education program had been completely ineffectual. Thus I decided to become a teacher educator so I could do a better job of preparing prospective teachers. I earned a doctorate at Indiana University and then taught in teacher-education programs at two colleges (Kansas State College of Pittsburg, Kansas, and San Francisco State College) before becoming a faculty member at the UCLA Graduate School of Education, where I taught for twenty-nine years. The first half of those nearly three decades at UCLA was focused on teacher education, but the last half centered on educational assessment because I'd learned by then that in a high-stakes testing environment, those who control the assessments have an enormous influence on what goes on instructionally in classrooms. In 1991, having discovered that emeritus (retired) professors received free campus parking, I took early retirement from UCLA. Since then, and because I have been released from all publish-or-perish shackles, I've been spending a good deal of time working with teachers to improve the instructional relevance of their classroom tests and with state-level officials to improve the caliber of their statewide accountability tests.

When I was young, I often sneered at experience, thinking that when a colleague invoked "my experience" in any sort of disagreement, it was often a sort of last-resort argument. Now, older and far more experienced, I realize that a lifetime of experiences—often laden with ample wrong turns—can put you in a position to share insights that are simply not apparent to less seasoned folks. And that's why I am writing this book. I've seen some serious mistakes made once and I'm seeing them made again. I now want those mistakes to be fixed, because it is high time for students to benefit from all six of the unlearned lessons to be treated in this book.

Let's get underway, then, with chapter 1 and the first unlearned lesson.

W. J. P.
January 2009

CHAPTER ONE

Too Many Curricular Targets

Most people are somewhat rational, at least on certain occasions. So, let's assume you happen to stumble onto one of these occasionally rational people, smack in a moment of unrelenting rationality. We'll assume she's a woman because—as my wife periodically informs me—females tend to be more clearheaded than males. Anyway, how do you think a rational woman, bristling with unclouded thoughts, would answer the question, "If an organization were trying to achieve a set of goals, how important would the nature of those goals be to the organization's success in attaining them?"

Assuming you've located a lucid lady who's atop her game, her answer ought to be something along these lines: "The nature of the goals an organization is pursuing will obviously have a profound impact on its success in achieving them." Most clear-thinking women—and men—readily recognize how significant the quality of an organization's intentions are to its achievements. Goals *do* make a difference: Stellar goals inspire organizations to achieve what's worthy. Trifling goals send organizations questing for the trivial. Then why are the goals we have established for our public schools so altogether irrational? At the moment, that's exactly what those goals are—completely irrational.

A HIGH-IMPORT PROBLEM, LARGELY UNRECOGNIZED

The first of the six unlearned lessons I'll be exploring in this book deals with a problem that may well be the most important of the lot. This initial lesson can be seen whenever educational policymakers require teachers to teach more things than time allows. To some, this might sound like a rather trifling mistake. After all, how many of us have gone to a buffet and put too much food on our plates? And how many people set out each weekend to accomplish more home-improvement tasks than they have time to complete? Over-filled plates and overly ambitious weekend plans are surely not a calamity—indeed, excessive aspirations don't seem like such a serious mistake. Yet when it comes to education, excessive curricular aspirations have an unforeseeable but devastating impact on educational quality. Moreover, for teachers, excessive curricular demands can become a bona fide instructional nightmare.

Surprisingly, however, few people regard the goals our schools are currently pursuing as constituting any sort of difficulty. To help you appreciate the nightmare today's overloaded teachers face, I need you do a bit of imagining. Suppose you're standing in the middle of a circular shooting gallery. On the walls surrounding you there are one hundred bulls-eye targets, each about twelve inches in diameter. You've been given a loaded handgun and told to hit all one hundred targets dead center. However—and here's where this situation gets bizarre—*you are only going to be allowed twenty seconds to do all of your shooting.*

You'll clearly not have time to make dead-center hits on all the targets. If you took really careful aim you might hit a few, but surely far fewer than required. If you aimed less carefully, you might hit more targets but almost certainly with less accuracy. And as if this scenario weren't bad enough, suppose you're told that only half of the targets will actually count—but you won't be told which ones until *after* you've finished your twenty seconds of shooting. This is surely a can't-win situation; fortunately, it is only make-believe. But how would you feel if, in real life, you were trapped in such an impossible situation? I know I'd be not only frustrated but seriously annoyed with whoever had placed me in such a pickle.

Sadly, many of today's teachers are facing similar work-related absurdity in their classrooms, and it's happening to them every single day. Their nightmare stems from the unreasonable requirement that they accomplish far more than is humanly possible during the instructional time available to them.

I've not actually ranked the relative seriousness of the problems currently facing American educators. However, if I were forced at gunpoint or enticed by a plateful of brownies to select the most important of all the problems currently vexing our schools—not just my six—I'd probably say that the most serious problem is that teachers are required to do more than they can conceivably do.

Curricular aims

Because the label "curriculum" means different things to different people, let me describe how I'll be using that term in this book. My view of curriculum is based on a simple distinction between ends and means. To me, curriculum refers to the ends or goals we want students to achieve—what we want our students to learn. On the other hand, instruction (or, if you prefer, teaching) is the means we employ to get students to achieve the curricular goals we've set for them. To illustrate, if students are supposed to learn long division, that's the curricular goal. In contrast, the activities the teacher employs to help students acquire the skill of long division represent the instructional means used to achieve that goal.

Through the years, numerous terms have been used to describe the curricular outcomes that teachers try to promote. When I began teaching high school during the mid-fifties, most educators referred to the things they wanted their students to learn as goals or, possibly, objectives. Goals tended to represent more general curricular aspirations; objectives were usually more specific. In recent years, however, what we referred to as goals have become known as content standards or, dressing them up a bit, academic content standards. And because most content standards tend to be fairly broad, they often subsume more specific curricular targets described as benchmarks, expectancies, outcomes, or some similar designation.

Because the label "curricular aim" has been used less frequently and, therefore, has had less time to have its meaning leeched out, I'll be using that term from here on to describe the skills, knowledge, or affect (attitudes, interests, and values) educators want their students to learn. Whereas most of today's curricular aims are cognitive (intellectual), a small number of them deal with psychomotor skills (such as using a computer keyboard) or affective outcomes (such as acquiring a positive attitude toward learning).

What's so vile about too many curricular aims?

At first glance, it may not seem so terrible for policymakers to lay out more curricular aims than can be taught in the time available. After all, isn't this simply an instance of one's eyes being bigger than one's stomach? Moreover, isn't it actually praiseworthy when policymakers set challenging goals for teachers? However, this mistake of having too many targets is more insidious than it might seem at first. Here's why.

A state's curricular aims are almost always used as a framework for its annual accountability tests. Today, students' scores on those tests are far and away the most dominant evidence of schools' instructional success. Thus, because educators understandably want their students to score well, they will tend to give instructional emphasis to whatever curricular aims are eligible to be assessed by their state's accountability tests. (In some states, any curricular aims that might be tested are clearly identified. In other states, all of the approved curricular aims are considered eligible for testing.)

It is apparent, then, that state-approved curricular aims have a considerable impact on what goes on in classrooms. If the number of curricular aims is reasonable and those aims are worthwhile, they will provide an effective focus for teachers' instructional efforts. If the number of curricular aims is excessive, as is usual these days, or if the aims are not defensible, as is sometimes the case, then the state's goals can subvert what might have been a successful educational program had more suitable curricular aims been in place.

One significant problem that too many curricular aims can engender is a coverage-quest climate, wherein teachers try to cover all the state's curricular targets, even if only superficially. We can sympathize with teachers who, having been given too many targets, decide to devote a perfunctory dash of attention to each curricular aim. Teachers who succumb to this approach are, in a sense, adopting a lick-and-a-promise strategy—except there's only time for a "lick," and the "promise" is rarely forthcoming. This cursory content coverage typically leads to what is, at best, short-duration learning, as curricular aims merely touched on by teachers rarely have any lasting impact on students. When America's schools are compared with those in other nations, it is often said that our curricular goals are a mile wide and an inch deep. Unfortunately, that's true.

A second, equally insidious shortcoming of having too many targets is associated with its impact on the accountability tests, which, as noted above, have considerable influence on instruction. Here's how this second difficulty arises.

Because there are far too many state-approved curricular aims, students' status regarding those aims cannot be accurately measured in the hour or so typically available for each accountability test. This is because it is usually necessary to employ at least a handful of items to determine whether a student has mastered a particular curricular aim. But there's not enough time to measure students' mastery of each target in a sprawling set of curricular aims—at least not in the sixty minutes or so available to test kids in, say, mathematics or reading. In fact, there often isn't time to devote even a single item to measuring some curriculum aims. So, the measurement companies that create the accountability tests are obliged to sample the curricular aims that are eligible to be tested. Some are not tested at all; some are tested with only one or two items; and few, if any, are tested with enough items to allow teachers to accurately determine whether a student has mastered the aim being assessed.

Again, because of the enormous importance these days of students' accountability test scores and because of teachers' preoccupation with having their students score well, many teachers guess which curricular aims will be assessed on a given test. Based on their guesses, teachers tend to emphasize certain curricular aims and deemphasize others, perhaps giving zero instructional attention to some. This kind of reaction to a galaxy of potential assessment targets is not outlandish; indeed, given the uncertainty of what will be assessed, guessing is about the only option open to teachers.

Sometimes, as you might expect, teachers will guess right. And, of course, sometimes they won't. In certain cases, a teacher will lavish attention on getting students to master a curricular aim that turns out not to be on that year's test. In other cases, a teacher will fail to give any instructional attention to a curricular aim that ends up being measured by quite a few test items. After several years of frustrating off-target guessing, many teachers simply stop giving any extra attention to curricular aims that might be measured by the accountability tests.

Although many teachers report that they're guided by what's to be measured on accountability tests, in the reality of their classrooms, when the door closes, they sometimes give little instructional attention to what's on the tests, except by accident. Many teachers, in a desperate effort to ready their students to perform well on the tests, rely on extensive, mind-numbing test-preparation activities that usually crowd out genuine instruction. Students spend hours and hours on test-prep drudgery because their teachers simply don't know what is going to be tested. Although the students might be learning lots about test-taking tactics, they also are often learning to despise school. This is too great a price to pay—teachers need to help students to acquire positive attitudes toward learning, not negative ones. The culprit in this particular curriculum caper is definitely the raw number of curricular targets. A more manageable number of curricular aims could help both teachers and students focus their efforts.

Summing up, then, in this nation we currently have a situation where almost all states are pursuing an unreasonable number of curricular aims. Because there is not time enough to teach what's represented by these excessive targets, and because students' mastery of those targets cannot be assessed in an instructionally sensible manner, the negative impact on U.S. classrooms is both pervasive and profound. Having too many curricular aims leads to off-target teaching and excessive test preparation and can, consequently, devastate a state's educational program. Although many of today's educators and educational policymakers remain ignorant of this problem, they really shouldn't be, as this ridiculous situation is far from new. If today's pursuit of too many curricular targets were not so blatantly harmful to students, it would be almost comical. But it *is* blatantly harmful and therefore definitely not comical.

THE BEHAVIORAL OBJECTIVES MOVEMENT

If you could turn back the clock on your personal time machine from the early part of the twenty-first century to the 1960s and early 1970s, you'd find there was considerable educational advocacy for what were then called behavioral objectives. I can tell you a bit about what was generally referred to as the behavioral objectives movement because I played a modest role in making it mobile.

Behavioral objectives were statements representing what teachers hoped students would know or be able to do when instruction was over.

By focusing explicitly on students' behavior, advocates of behavioral objectives attempted to dodge the fuzzy language found in most curricular aims in the first half of the twentieth century—language that often laid out such murky goals as:

- The student will understand the fundamental nature of the American Revolution.
- Students will become familiar with the literary strategies and tactics linked to the major genres of written composition.
- Learners will learn to relish literature.

My favorite objective of that era is the third, which calls for learners to "relish literature." I actually encountered this objective years ago in a district curriculum guide for language arts. Ever since, I have been on the lookout for an objective urging students to "mayonnaise mathematics." To date, unfortunately, I have not yet run into a mayo-math objective.

As you can see, before the introduction of behavioral objectives, many curricular aims were stated so generally that it was practically impossible to determine whether students had actually achieved them. The way most objectives were articulated reduced them to little more than heartfelt hopes for students to attain worthwhile, albeit nebulous, outcomes. But then, in the early 1960s, the proponents of behavioral objectives sauntered stridently onto the scene.

Programmed instruction as a spur

During the late 1950s and 1960s, there was considerable excitement among U.S. educators regarding the potential educational payoffs of programmed instruction and, particularly, teaching machines. Programmed instruction involved arranging printed instructional materials into carefully sequenced segments, which were then tried out with small groups of students so they could be revised if necessary, based on those students' postinstruction test performances. The revised materials were then tried out with more students, and this cycle was repeated until the programmed materials worked satisfactorily. At that point, the materials were presented to learners via a mechanical device called a teaching machine, or in a "programmed book." The teaching machines doled out tasks to students using mechanical or electronic procedures, provided a place for them to respond, and then indicated whether the responses were correct. Programmed books did roughly the same thing, obliging students to make their responses on one page and then turn to another to see if their responses were correct. Because the idea of having students taught by machines rather than by teachers was obviously innovative, teaching machines and programmed instruction garnered lots of attention from the popular press.

Much of the early work with programmed instruction and teaching machines was influenced by the pioneering work of B. F. Skinner, the behavioral psychologist whose research on the modification of animal behavior through positive reinforcement was well known at the time. Skinner devised his own teaching machines and the instructional materials that went into them. He even authored a programmed book dealing with the principles of general psychology. Because of his belief in the importance of students' responses being positively reinforced, Skinner's programming approach moved students forward in exceedingly small steps by posing incrementally more difficult questions. Thus, when responding to a Skinnerian program's slightly tougher questions, the students were almost invariably be correct and would typically be reinforced by "being right." This small-step-by-small-step approach, which was the key feature of Skinner's strategy, was described as linear programming.

Other programming strategies during that era were designed to adapt to the styles of different learners. They presented sometimes substantially different sequences of instructional materials based on the way students responded to each question—typically multiple-choice questions—throughout the program. Because of the potential diversity in the sequence of instructional materials a learner might encounter, these approaches were generally described as branching programs.

But whether linear or branching, the most critical component of the programmed instruction process was the assessment evidence that indicated whether students had actually learned what they had been taught. This requirement clearly obliged the creators of programmed instruction to think through carefully, in advance, precisely what their hoped-for outcomes were. Once these programmers had a good fix on what their materials were supposed to accomplish, they could build tests that would indicate whether a particular version of a program had worked well or whether another revision would be required. Accordingly, objectives for students, fashioned in a measurable form, became a sine qua non of programmed instruction during the late fifties and early sixties.

In 1961, Robert Mager, an instructional researcher at Varian Associates (an electronics firm located south of San Francisco), began writing a brief book about how to construct objectives for programmed instruction. Mager wanted to write this book because he realized that properly formulated objectives were at the heart of any sensible programmed instruction approach. At that time, I was a faculty member at San Francisco State College and had just begun teaching a new course about teaching machines and programmed instruction. I knew Mager well, so when he asked to try out a draft of his new book in my course, I was more than willing. Besides, the book itself was programmed, written in a branching format, so by reading his book my students would learn more about how to write objectives while using a popular programming strategy.

Although this tryout of Mager's book took place many years ago, I can still recall sitting with him in the back of the classroom, watching my students go through his draft materials. At one point he turned to me and said, "When all the excitement about teaching machines and programmed instruction has died down, what educators will ultimately get out of this movement is a heightened appreciation of the importance of stating instructional objectives more clearly." History has proven him correct.

One year later, in 1962, Mager's book was published. It was called *Preparing Objectives for Programmed Instruction*. Subsequent editions were simply called *Preparing Instructional Objectives*. That slender little volume had a substantial impact on the way American educators thought about formulating their instructional intentions. Mager showed educators how to write an instructional objective so that it spelled out students' post-instruction behavior. In other words, according to Mager, a behavioral objective described the observable behaviors (such as completing a written test or making an oral presentation) that would allow educators to determine whether a student had acquired some desired intellectual skill or body of knowledge.

Some examples of the kinds of behavioral objectives that were attracting so much attention in the early sixties follow. You will note that in addition to specifying the desired behavior, these objectives also established

SIDEBAR 1.1
Skinnerian Scenario

In 1977–78, I was president of the American Educational Research Association (AERA), an international organization of education researchers. Sometime during the winter months, I received a telephone call at UCLA from Bill Russell, our association's executive officer. Explaining that a key AERA awards committee had chosen B. F. Skinner to be the recipient of an important award, Bill asked me if I'd call Professor Skinner to see if he would be willing to receive the award at the upcoming annual meeting of AERA in Toronto. A condition of the award was that the recipient had to receive it in person and make a brief presentation to the AERA members. The award was to be accompanied by a fairly sizeable check, but the committee was worried that Skinner would not come to Toronto to accept it.

I had met Skinner on only one occasion, but I knew his work well. He was, and is, generally conceded to be "the father of behavior modification." I had been a fan since I was a graduate student, having read most of his pioneering works about how to modify the behavior of subhuman organisms using both positive and negative reinforcement. I had, by that time, already read Skinner's novel, *Walden II,* twice. I really admired this man.

So, with considerable apprehension, I telephoned Skinner's office at Harvard to extend the invitation. I was surprised when he answered the phone himself, but I proceeded with enthusiasm to tell him of the award, to congrat-

the level of proficiency at which a student ought to be able to display that behavior:

- Students will be able to write an original expository essay of at least one thousand words in which there are no more than five errors in punctuation, spelling, or grammar.
- Students will be able to calculate the correct answers to 80 percent or more of twenty randomly generated multiplication problems involving pairs of double-digit numbers.
- When presented with oral or written descriptions of major political conflicts in American history, the learner will be able to accurately identify, from a set of twenty-five key historical events, (such as the

ulate him effusively, and then to invite him to come to Toronto in the spring to receive the award. He turned me down cold.

Skinner explained that he was deeply involved in writing the second volume of his autobiography and just didn't have the time to travel. Though deeply disappointed, I took advantage of this rare opportunity to talk a bit more with a professor I idolized. I asked him how his second autobiographical volume was coming and told him I had read volume one, and I brought up several of his more significant experiments. He was most cordial, but any time I tried to bring up his attending the Toronto conference, he deftly dodged my overtures.

Then, after having chatted with him cordially for about twenty minutes, I flashed on an idea. Pausing for a moment, I said, "Dr. Skinner, you live in Cambridge, Massachusetts. That's really only a short plane ride from Toronto, and we always have our award sessions in the evenings. You could hop onto an afternoon plane, take part in the awards ceremony, stay the night in Canada, and grab a morning flight back to Boston. You could be back at your writing by mid-morning." He paused for what seemed like a decade, then replied, "Yes, I guess I could to that. Okay, I'll be there."

I was slightly ecstatic for just a bit, and then the majesty of the moment enveloped me. *I had modified the behavior of B. F. Skinner!*

Epilogue: Professor Skinner did attend the session, bringing with him his original teaching machine—a device that now sits in one of the nation's major museums—and gave a wonderful 20-minute address to several thousand AERA members. It was a special night in Toronto.

Civil War and the Industrial Revolution) with at least 90 percent accuracy, the event with which each conflict was associated.

One of Mager's contributions to the way educators stated their instructional objectives was his recommendation that, whenever possible, behavioral objectives contain minimum expectations for both classes and individual students. A minimum level for students specifies how well an individual must be able to display the behavior called for in the objective. A minimum level for a class stipulates what percentage of the students would need to perform at or above the specified student minimum level. The above examples of behavioral objectives only include minimum levels for students. If we were to add minimum levels for the class, here's what they would look like (the class minimum levels are in italics):

- A *minimum of 75 percent of the students* will be able to write an original expository essay of at least one thousand words in which there are no more than five errors in punctuation, spelling, or grammar.
- *At least 90 percent of the students* will be able to calculate the correct answers to 80 percent or more of twenty randomly generated multiplication problems involving pairs of double-digit numbers.
- When presented with oral or written descriptions of political conflicts in American history, *all* learners will be able to accurately identify, from a set of twenty-five key historical events (such as the Civil War and the Industrial Revolution) with at least 90 percent accuracy, the event with which each conflict was associated.

Because behavioral objectives represented more explicit descriptions of what educators wanted for their students and even set forth the minimally acceptable levels of performance for both individuals and groups, they were regarded by many educators as a genuine advance in the rigor of our instructional thinking. I was one of those educators.

Behavioral objectives gain a midwife

Michael Scriven, the well-known educational evaluator, once described me as "the licensed midwife to the birth of behavioral objectives in the United States." Well, I definitely never acquired the requisite license, but for well over a decade I was pushing plenty hard for American teachers to adopt behavioral objectives.

Put simply, I believed strongly in the instructional dividends derived from the clarity of instructional intent embodied in behavioral objectives. I assumed, back in the early sixties, that the more clearly teachers understood what their students were supposed to be able to do after instruction, the more likely it was they could devise on-target activities for their students. As a consequence of that belief—a belief to which I adhere even today—I set out to promote the use of behavioral objectives among U.S. educators. I wrote articles and books advocating their use. I gave scads of speeches with the same message. I even developed a film-strip-audiotape program for in-service educators about how to create behavioral objectives. That particular program was, hands-down, the most popular of its type during the mid-sixties. It reached thousands of educators and was even translated into Spanish and used in many parts of Latin America. At UCLA, where I was teaching large numbers of prospective teachers (about a thousand each year), I gave each of my students a blue-and-gold bumper sticker saying, HELP STAMP OUT NONBEHAVIORAL OBJECTIVES! Yes, I was definitely into advocating behavioral objectives.

My own zeal for behavioral objectives notwithstanding, it was actually the Elementary and Secondary Education Act of 1965 (ESEA) that spurred their widespread adoption across America. That key law, a major element of President Lyndon Johnson's Great Society, was the precursor of its 2002 reauthorization, the No Child Left Behind Act (NCLB). ESEA was inarguably a precedent-setting law because, as never before, it called for major federal dollars to be doled out to states, which in turn dispensed those funds to local districts. In order to get the next year's share of this federal largesse, district educators throughout the nation tried to do whatever seemed to be favored by federal education officials. And guess what? A number of federal education officials at that time definitely grooved on behavioral objectives.

Thus, the regulations associated with a number of programs funded by ESEA urged educators to formulate their instructional intentions for these federally subsidized programs in a form that allowed external evaluators (such as federal officials) to determine if the program had actually been successful. In the years immediately following ESEA's enactment, federal authorities pushed hard for local educators to adopt behavioral objectives.

That push was so strong, in fact, that when I was on the road giving speeches in support of behavioral objectives, I frequently encountered school districts whose leaders were planning to have their educators spell out behavioral objectives for all (or most) subject areas and at all (or most) grade levels. In 1968, just after I had given back-to-back speeches about the raptures of behavioral objectives to educators in two school districts——Fresno, California, and Clark County, Nevada—administrators in both districts, under pressure to come up with behavioral

SIDEBAR 1.2

An Ethiopian Realization

During the middle 1960s, UCLA was actively involved in training Peace Corps Volunteers (PCVs) to serve as teachers in foreign nations. We prepared prospective teachers for Nigeria, Ethiopia, and a number of Central American countries. I was the UCLA professor in charge of the instructional methods part of that training, so in the courses I taught for the PCVs, I always stressed the need for them to spell out their objectives in behavioral form. Once these teachers-in-training had identified their behavioral objectives, then and only then did I allow them to create the daily and long-term lesson plans that would help their students attain the objectives the volunteers had identified. Behavioral objectives, I stressed, were the cornerstones of clear instructional thinking. It was an exciting time for me, chiefly because the volunteers were uniformly bright, motivated risk-takers. From my perspective, they were simply a delight.

So when I got a call from Washington, D.C., and was asked if I would be willing to spend three weeks in Ethiopia visiting the classrooms of PCV teachers I'd help train six months earlier, I quickly accepted. I was being asked to see how the instructional advice given in our UCLA teacher-training program was playing out in Ethiopia. Within a month, I was in Ethiopia.

After spending about two weeks visiting PCVs in their homes and classrooms, I headed to a town south of Addis Ababa called Yirga Alem. Two volunteers were teaching in the high school there. As always before going to one

objectives, enthusiastically informed me that they were about to create behavioral objectives for mathematics in grades 5 through 9.

Although I was pleased with these educators' commitment to generate proper objectives, it offended me that tax dollars and educators' precious time would be wasted in what was certain to be a case of reinventing the wheel. Why should two school districts separately carve out behavioral objectives for precisely the same subject area at precisely the same grade levels? Surely, mathematics in grades 5 and 9 were not all that different for kids in Fresno than for kids in Clark County. (On second thought, because Las Vegas is located in Clark County, there just might be some differences in the way teachers there are supposed to deal with lucky numbers such as 7, 11, and 21.)

of these sites, I looked up the PCVs in a roster book we had used during training that fortunately contained small mugshots of all the volunteers in training. Because the PCVs in Ethiopia had not been told that I would be visiting them, my arrival typically brought a predictable degree of surprise.

So, when I found myself walking down a dusty road in Yirga Alem and saw one of the volunteers, I was able, thanks to the roster book, to call out to him by name. Astonished to find a UCLA prof wandering down an Ethiopian road, he obviously recognized me but, just as obviously, couldn't recall my name. Hesitating only for a moment and producing a wide grin, he greeted me by saying, "Dr. Objectives, welcome!"

I was pleased that he had apparently retained at least one of the key messages I'd been hammering on back at UCLA, so when we went back to his hut (it was fashionable at that time for PCVs in Ethiopia to live in huts), I asked him if he really recalled the information about instruction objectives. Lighting up, he said, "Absolutely! I think behavioral objectives are great. I especially liked the distinction among cognitive, affective, and psychomotor objectives!"

Delighted that he clearly had a good handle on the topic, I asked him whether behavioral objectives were proving useful in his teaching. His reply, however, dismayed me more than a little. Smiling mischievously, he looked me straight in the eye and said, "I don't use behavioral objectives, Dr. Popham. I'm too damn busy teaching!"

I realized at that moment in Yirga Alem, theory had bumped into practice. And practice had won.

Within a few days of those speeches, I proposed to leaders of the UCLA Center for the Study of Evaluation that we establish a clearing house for behavioral objectives so American educators in pursuit of such objectives would not be obliged to create them from scratch. In late 1968, the Instructional Objectives Exchange (IOX) was established at UCLA, and by late 1969, IOX was offering more than a dozen collections of behavioral objectives along with illustrative test items to measure students' attainment of those objectives. Within a few years, IOX made available more than fifty collections of behavioral objectives and sample test items.

By the early seventies, the U.S. behavioral objectives movement had peaked. Most schools and districts by that time had begun specifying their instructional intentions in the form of behavioral objectives, and relatively few schools and districts still presented their curricular aims in fuzzy language. Behavioral objectives, clearly, had caught on.

But those of us who gleefully pounded the behavioral objectives drum had, regrettably, made a serious mistake: we had equated specificity with utility. We thought that the more specifically an instructional objective set forth what students were supposed to learn to be able to do, the more useful this objective would be to teachers. Clearer intent, we assumed, would lead to more insightful planning and, subsequently, to more on-target delivery of instruction. What we messed up on—and it was a major mess-up—was that we were advocating for the use of objectives written at the wrong grain size.

The grain size of an instructional objective refers to the breadth of the outcome teachers seek from their students. An example of large grain size would be when a student can generate an original, effective, persuasive essay. That's a significant instructional outcome, and it might take a full semester or school year for students to accomplish it. An objective with a small grain size might deal with a less demanding outcome, such being able to correctly spell all the words in a set of thirty "spelling demons." Objectives with such small grain size might be achieved in a single class period. During the sixties, advocates of behavioral objectives ended up recommending so many small-grain objectives that we overwhelmed the nation's educators. It was a profound error.

For example, some of the collections of behavioral objectives distributed nationally by the IOX contained hundreds of small-grain objectives. I recall a couple of collections of math and language arts objectives for elementary schools that included more than three hundred objectives *each!* There were simply too many behavioral objectives for any sensible teacher to tackle.

By the late seventies and early eighties, fewer and fewer educators advocated the use of behavioral objectives. Too many were already out there in the form of over-crowded sets of tiny state or district instructional objectives. Astute educators began to slink away from the bandwagon that had, only a few years earlier, pretty much represented the way educators were supposed to play the curricular game. I accept my share of the responsibility for not recognizing much sooner that we were pushing for objectives crafted in the wrong grain size. In retrospect, I wish desperately that I had been much smarter much sooner.

But American educators should have learned from that experience. We should have realized that having an excessive number of curricular aims is always counterproductive. Thus, when the standards movement became fashionable in American education in the late eighties and early nineties, we should have realized instantly that listing almost endless numbers of instructional objectives—now being called content standards—was every bit as dumb as it had been several decades earlier. It was a lesson educators definitely should have learned, but we did not. This unlearned lesson is now causing America's public schools to serve our nation's children less well than they should.

A LESSON-LEARNT SOLUTION

Anytime most of us hear someone comment on just about anything with a British accent, we instantly assume their view is meritorious. Visions of Shakespeare, the Magna Carta, and Rudyard Kipling dance in our heads. That's because British-accented comments seem so, well, *British*. When Brits use the past tense of the word learn, they often employ "learnt" rather than "learned." I have opted to use the classy BBC version of the past tense as I lay out my solutions to the six problems considered in this book. For the first problem—namely, the profusion of curricular aims currently messing up our schools—I think there is a straightforward solution, and it is definitely time that the behavioral objectives movement's sorry lesson was properly *learnt*.

From whence come curricular aims?

Before digging into the details of my solution, I need to make it clear where curricular aims come from in the first place. Although teachers can, at least to some extent, decide on a set of curricular aims for their students, almost all sensible teachers pay attention to the "official" aims issued by their state or school district because the accountability tests most states administer are meant to measure students' mastery of state-sanctioned content standards. And, of course, students' scores on these tests are currently seen as the most important indicator of a teacher's instructional success. Accordingly, most teachers will try to get their students to master what has been set forth by the state. It is apparent, then, that a state's official curricular aims—if assessed by an annual accountability test—will have a substantial impact on what really takes place in the classroom.

It is an educational truism that what gets tested gets taught, and the more important the tests are, the more certain it is that teachers will focus on what is to be tested. But where do these influential curricular aims come from in the first place?

State curricular aims are almost always initially identified by curriculum advisory committees composed of experienced teachers, other subject-matter experts such as university professors, and national subject-matter consultants. Actually, these committees often only recommend curricular aims for their particular fields, and those aims become official only after they are formally approved by an authorized policymaking group such as a state board of education or a state legislature. Typically, state-level curriculum advisory committees meet periodically for several weeks or months to consider potential curricular aims. They often consult the curricular recommendations of state or national subject-matter groups, such as the National Council of Teachers of Mathematics, most of which have issued recommendations regarding appropriate curricular choices in their area of specialty.

State-level curriculum advisory committees typically indicate what skills, knowledge, or affective outcomes students are supposed to acquire at each grade level or, perhaps, by the end of certain grade ranges—for instance, grades K–3, 4–6, 7–9, and 10–12—in the subject specialty for which they are responsible. An advisory committee in language arts might identify the state's curricular aims in both reading and composition, or there might be separate committees dealing only with reading and only with written composition. The composition of such committees and their subject-area responsibilities are typically determined by state officials, and although there are minor differences between states, most such committees are composed of similar individuals and undertake similar missions; namely, to figure out what kids need to learn at each grade level.

I have personally observed a number of these committees as they wrestle with the challenge of defining a defensible set of grade-appropriate curricular aims for their state's students. Committee members are typically bright, well-intentioned, knowledgeable educators, and I have never seen them tackle their task with anything but a resolute determination to do what's best for kids. Nonetheless, these advisory committees invariably blunder—and they blunder big time! They make a mistake that profoundly cripples education in their states. Simply put, they ask teachers to teach much too much.

You see, curriculum committee members are almost always subject-matter specialists who are chosen for their expertise in the subject being addressed. Why ask a teacher to serve on a math committee if that teacher's math ability tops out at adding or subtracting single-digit numbers? No, educators are asked to sit on a curriculum advisory committee only if they have indisputable content expertise. Paradoxically, this laudable quality usually lands such committees in Trouble City.

Here's what almost always happens when curriculum committees get around to the nitty-gritty of deciding which skills, knowledge, and affective outcomes should be instructional targets for their students. As the committees consider various curricular aims, they draw on their experience to determine which aims can and should be achieved at different grade levels by students of particular ages. This is an altogether reasonable way of tackling the question of what to teach.

However, when reviewing potential curricular aims, these committees typically decide that students should learn "almost everything" about a particular subject. This is an understandable consequence of asking specialists to identify what they want students to learn, because most specialists love their own field.

Having served as the moderator for this sort of session on numerous occasions, I have often seen two committee members push to include substantially different curricular aims. What often happened was that the two reached a compromise—basically, "You vote for my curricular aim and I'll vote for yours." Thus, in striving to maintain cordial relations, curricular skirmishes almost always ended up with both aims being approved. Due to such mutual back-scratching, the curricular aims embraced by advisory committees often multiplied more rapidly than rodents.

When advisory committees opt for a large number of curricular aims, the resulting targets constitute less of a realistic set of educational goals and more of an unadulterated wish list. The avalanche of curricular aims recommended by almost all state-level advisory committees reflects what the committee members wish students knew about a subject area rather than what can be taught and tested in the time available. Therefore, elementary teachers in many states are asked to have their students master an enormous number of curricular aims. In some states, high school teachers are required to get their students to achieve more than one hundred curricular aims during a single semester. This is simply silly. And yet, when the recommendations of a curriculum advisory committee are forwarded to an official decisionmaking group (such as a state school board), those recommendations are almost always approved. It is apparently assumed that whatever emerges from these specialized committees warrants approval. This assumption is largely untenable because curriculum advisory committees almost always want teachers to teach too much stuff.

In California, for example, state regulations require a fourth-grade teacher to get students to master 112 curricular aims in mathematics and language arts alone. And when other subjects such as science, social studies, and the arts are tossed in, the number rises to 299. Absurd!

This sort of curricular profusion is the rule, not the exception. California is typical of other states, although curricular aims elsewhere may be labeled differently and some states may seem to have only a small number. For example, certain states list only a half-dozen content standards, but those six are typically so broadly defined that any kind of curricular clarity is cloaked. Teachers often can't tell what such broad curricular aims actually mean. For instance, a state might have only one geometry content standard in mathematics, but when the state gets around to spelling out what geometry skills are subsumed under this broad label, there may be twenty or thirty targets. What teachers need is curricular targets described so specifically that teachers can readily translate them into classroom instruction. When there are too many targets, problems erupt.

Advisory committees are rarely warned of the perils in recommending too many curricular targets. Rarely are they obliged to prioritize their curricular preferences. Rarely are they apprised of the serious negative effect that having too many curricular aims can have on accountability tests and on what goes on instructionally in classrooms. And these groups almost never delete an item from a list of curricular contenders. They seem to believe that if they identify huge numbers of curricular targets, those targets will be addressed successfully by teachers. Nothing could be less true. Hoped-for curricular outcomes—even those determined by knowledgeable content specialists—are not instantly relayed by zealous teachers and do not scamper into students' skulls. Too many curriculum targets, in truth, turn out to be no targets at all.

The solution's essence

The way to get out of the problem of having too many curricular aims is simple. What needs to be done is to formulate all potential curricular aims at an appropriate grain size and then prioritize those targets so they can be both tested and taught properly. The heart of this proposed solution, then, is prioritizing properly sized curricular aims. Let's see how this solution would work in practice.

First, because most states have invested considerable money and time in identifying their content standards, those standards could be left untouched. Although typically too numerous, the standards represent the schooling outcomes that a committee of experts hope the state's students will accomplish. Accordingly, most such collections set forth worthwhile goals that educators would do well to consider.

State educators could fundamentally revise their content standards, of course, but there is no immediate need to do so. However, educational policymakers should prioritize the most important curricular aims and then assess students' mastery of them via an annual accountability test. Because of the importance of students' performance on accountability tests, these curricular aims would receive considerable attention in the classroom.

Second, the curriculum targets to be assessed each year must be formulated at an appropriate grain size, or breadth; therefore, an appropriate grain size for the curricular aims would generally be fairly large. They would need to be broad enough so there were not too many, but not so broad that their meaning was obscured. An excellent illustration of a curricular aim with a suitable grain size can be found in language arts when we ask our students to become proficient writers. It might be framed along these lines:

> Students will be able to write original essays representing any of the follow-
> ing composition genres: exposition, narration, persuasion, or description.

This curricular aim represents a powerful set of writing skills, which are readily measurable by asking students to create a writing sample to demonstrate that they can, in fact, generate suitable compositions representing the four genres identified. Each of those writing skills, of course, subsumes a set of subskills (such as ways to organize content for different writing genres) and enabling knowledge (such as memorizing prominent punctuation and usage conventions). Thus, when teachers are asked to focus at least part of their instruction on getting students to master this potent curricular aim, they will have a reasonably clear notion of what students are supposed to be able to do when instruction is over.

Typically, the large-grain curricular aims that represent a state's high-priority goals focus on students' cognitive skills rather than on their knowledge acquisition. Having students acquire knowledge is important, of course, but knowledge can support students' acquisition of higher-order cognitive skills. When educators have a limited number of curricular targets, it is more sensible to regard students' acquisition of knowledge as a building block underlying their mastery of broader cognitive skills.

Remember, the creation of an assessment framework based on a state's existing curricular aims will not replace those aims. An assessment framework presents more defensible high-priority curricular targets formulated at a suitable grain size. Educators are free to lavish as much attention on any nonassessed curricular target as they wish. Indeed, if the assessment framework is properly conceptualized, it should nurture instruction that is not only successful but efficient. Efficient instruction allows teachers to promote students' mastery of state-assessed curricular targets as rapidly as possible, thereby freeing up instructional time for them to tackle as many nonassessed but official curricular aims as possible.

The installation of more manageable, properly sized, high-priority curricular aims as a framework for a state's accountability assessments need not narrow its curriculum. Remember, by reconceptualizing the most important curricular aims at a larger grain size, these larger curricular targets will often subsume a number of aims that are smaller in scope. It is also important to remember that many lesser state curricular aims will never be given anything more than cursory instructional attention. Coalescing lesser skills and knowledge with properly sized, high-priority curricular aims doesn't shrink what is to be taught. It represents, rather, an honest, unembellished picture of what teachers can actually accomplish.

Dollops of distress

The seriousness of this problem is obscured by the trivial amount of attention it has received. In truth, any serious-minded discussion of the glut of curricular aims we now find in the United States, no matter how carefully those aims were crafted, would surely identify the inherent foolishness of setting out more goals to teach (and test) than there is time available to teach (or test). And yet, perhaps because we derive some sort of satisfaction from putting grandiose wishes on paper, the problem of excessive curricular aspirations has rarely received attention from either educators or non-educators. Happily, in recent years, we occasionally encounter murmurs of dismay with our present profusion of curricular aims.

For example, when the state of Oregon commissioned WestEd, a major nonprofit research and development organization, to evaluate the state assessment system and curricular aims,[1] WestEd's evaluators concluded that a major shortcoming of Oregon's approach to accountability was its excessive number of curricular targets. Stanley Rabinowitz, an architect of the WestEd analysis, observed that the Oregon Department of Education "may want to consider a new standards structure that includes only a limited number of high priority standards."[2] And, in a recent book about how to make content standards useful in the classroom, Marzano and Haystead argue that "state and national standards articulate far too much content."[3]

Traveling from state to state these days, one sometimes hears educators' requests for the state content standards to be prioritized. Education officials in Pennsylvania have attempted in recent years to identify their most significant content standards, thereby marking them as likely to be assessed annually. Indiana's education leaders have made similar serious efforts to winnow what will be assessed by their state's accountability tests.[4]

Because many people, educators included, are loath to discard almost anything, some educators are clearly reluctant to toss out any curricular aims. It seems that if educators jettison any worthwhile curricular targets, students are certain to be educationally shortchanged. But in prioritizing a set of curricular aims, there is no reason to toss out those ranked lower, as they can be addressed instructionally if time permits. What is more crucial, however, is that the high-priority curricular aims can be taught in sufficient depth to be mastered by students, and because their numbers will be more manageable they can be properly assessed. Teachers, students, and students' parents will be able to tell which curricular aims students have and haven't mastered. This is a truly important consideration if we wish to educate our children properly.

Although the voices registering dissent with today's crammed curriculum are currently little more than a whisper, just a few years ago such whispers were rarely heard. As more and more thoughtful people begin to recognize the indefensibility of our current curricular formulations, we may achieve sufficient protests to spur corrective action regarding our overabundance of curricular aims.

An example of an assessment framework in reading

One challenge in framing curricular aims at a suitable grain size requires applying the "Goldilocks Rule"—curricular aims that are not too broad and not too narrow, but *just right*. It is typically easier to offer guidance than to come up with curricular aims that are just the right size, therefore it will often be necessary to coalesce a narrow set of curricular aims into a broader, more comprehensive target. Care must be taken that the grain size does not become so large that it loses clarity. The following are two examples of aims written at an overly large grain size:

> Students will acquire all necessary knowledge regarding pivotal events in the history of the United States of America.

> Students in every mathematics class will become proficient solvers of diverse quantitative problems.

Such excessively broad curricular aims may sound impressive, but they fail to communicate accurately—to teachers, students, or parents—just what students are supposed to learn.

In 2002, Roger Farr, an Indiana University reading professor of international prominence, attempted to rework the numerous curricular aims in reading so that a more manageable set could emerge. Farr called his concept *purposeful reading* because, he argued, good readers not only always read for a purpose, they also should have a purpose in mind when they read anything. Farr reasoned, therefore, that students should be taught from their earliest school days to read for a purpose. He divided the kinds of reading materials people encounter into three categories: functional texts (such as a bus or train schedule), expository texts (such as an essay or an encyclopedia entry), and narrative texts (such as a short story or novel). Farr identified the chief reasons people read each sort of written material. When he was through, there were only eight fundamental purpose-focused skills a reader really needed to possess. One of Farr's eight skills—students can read to select and apply relevant information for a given purpose—illustrates a reason for reading functional texts. For example, a reader has a particular purpose in mind (such as figuring out when the next bus leaves for home), then has to select the needed information from a suitable functional text and, having done so, must satisfy the intended purpose (determining when the appropriate bus leaves).

In life, people bring their own purposes to what they read. To assess students' acquisition of this skill, however, test items would typically supply a given purpose—for example, by employing such language as, "Suppose you were reading the movie guide below in order to determine the times when it would be least expensive to see newly released films, in general when should you try to go to the movies if you want to save money on ticket prices?"

Farr's eight reading skills, then, constitute all of the major curricular aims in reading that are to be assessed by accountability tests. Because there are only eight skills, these tests can readily include sufficient items to measure each one so that teachers, students, and parents can tell which skills students have and haven't mastered. This, then, is an example of how existing curricular aims can be reconceptualized at a more suitable grain size so that the high-priority aims can be accurately assessed each year. The state of Wyoming, incidentally, has adopted Farr's innovative framework as accountability targets in K–12 reading.

Assessment considerations

To help teachers focus their instruction on having students master significant skills—that is, the sorts of cognitive skills that will serve students well throughout school and beyond—it is important for those who create assessment frameworks to generate descriptive materials that spell out the nature of the curricular aim being sought and assessed. Typically, in a page or two of descriptive information that includes sample tests items, state officials can communicate to teachers the precise nature of a skill that will be assessed. With such descriptions in hand, teachers can aim their instruction at students' mastering skills rather than their answering particular test items correctly. The Wyoming Department of Education gives its teachers such descriptions for all state-assessed curricular aims. (You can read more about this in chapter 7.)

The only legitimate reason for state-level educational testing is to improve teachers' instruction and thereby enhance students' learning. But this means that state tests must contain sufficient items for each curricular aim in order to determine the degree to which each student has, in fact, achieved the targeted aims. Earlier in the chapter I described the educational mischief that can arise when, because of having to assess too many curricular aims, there is no room on tests to accurately measure students' status on each aim. This can breed off-target teaching or excessive test preparation, which is why prioritizing the curricular aims a state will assess is absolutely critical.

Put simply, today's incomplete and often misleading measurement of students' mastery of curricular aims makes no sense. Only those curricular aims we can accurately assess—with enough items—should be on the to-be-assessed list.

The number of items needed to determine students' mastery will, of course, vary according to the nature of the aims. Some will be broader than others and require more items per aim. In other instances, such as when measuring how well students can compose an essay, it may be sufficient to have students produce only one or two essays. After all, if a student can crank out a satisfactory persuasive essay on one occasion, isn't it likely the student can do so again? A good way to determine how many items it might take to accurately judge a student's status regarding different curricular aims is to ask a group of seasoned teachers to estimate the number of items needed for each curricular aim.

When determining how many items it will take to arrive at an instructionally informative estimate of a student's mastery of particular curricular aims; this determination centers on what measurement specialists describe as validity. Assessment validity refers to the accuracy of the inferences we make about students based on their test performance. So, for curricular aims with larger grain size—that is, for curricular aims dealing with broader skills or bodies of knowledge—it will usually take more test items for teachers to make an accurate judgment of a given student's mastery of a particular curricular aim.

Of course, we must set a realistic limit on the number of items we should use to arrive at valid inferences regarding student performance. For example, we don't need to have students answer one hundred items about subtracting numbers. Experienced teachers will usually make sensible judgments about how many items are needed, but unless there are enough items to get a meaningful sense of a student's mastery, there isn't any sense in assessing them. Measuring students' mastery of a curricular aim with too few items and then claiming that measurement is accurate constitutes something dangerously close to assessment fraud.

This is why prioritizing curricular aims is so important. The number of curricular aims that can be assessed by a state accountability test must be no greater than the number of curricular aims for which there can be a sufficient number of items to determine each student's mastery of each curricular aim. Again, this is why it is important to aim for the right grain size when selecting the curricular aims for any assessment framework. The larger the grain size the better—as long as the curricular aims do not become too large to describe sensibly.

Remember, in creating assessment frameworks we are not diminishing the hopes we have for our children. No, we need not narrow the curricular targets we have for our students. Rather, we are laying out with honesty the assessment targets that represent what can actually be accomplished in our schools. Honesty is a useful attribute of any curricular strategy intended to benefit children.

CHAPTER TWO

The Underutilization of Classroom Assessment

If a surgical scalpel is only used to spread cream cheese on crackers, it is being profoundly underutilized. Similarly, when teachers use classroom tests only to grade their students, those tests are also being profoundly underutilized. Underutilization is a particularly common error of omission. But a mistake being common does not make it excusable. Tools or procedures tend to be underutilized because no one has figured out how to use them more fully. Nonetheless, such errors of omission can be every bit as harmful as their often more visible cousins, errors of commission.

In this chapter, I'll consider another of the six unlearned lessons addressed in this book. This second mistake stems from teachers' profound underutilization of classroom assessment. It is a pervasive error of omission that impedes many students' progress in school.

Classroom assessments, as I will explain, are tools that, if employed properly, can have a powerful and positive impact on students' learning. Unfortunately, in most schools today, classroom assessments are not being used properly, which constitutes a colossal error of omission for the kids involved.

THE TRADITIONAL ROLE OF CLASSROOM TESTS

Before digging more deeply into the nature of this chapter's lesson, let's make sure we agree on what educators mean by "classroom assessment."

To most educators it describes a wide array of tools and techniques for gathering evidence, not merely the paper-and-pencil tests that most of us adults experienced as we went through school. Moreover, most educators today tend to use the term "assessments" rather than "tests" because tests conjures up images of the conventional type of exams we've seen in schools for decades. So, while it is not a monumental gaffe to say classroom testing, most educators prefer the broader label of classroom assessment, which is the term I will use from this point forward.

When teachers employ any type of assessment approach, they are using students' overt performance to get a fix on their covert skills and knowledge. Let's face it, teachers can't tell how well students can read merely by looking at them. A student's ability to read, to compose an essay, or to determine a square root is an unseen attribute lurking someplace inside the student's skull. So, in order to determine how well students can, say, write a narrative essay, teachers ask them to actually compose one. Based on a student's overt performance—that is, the writing sample—the teacher can make an inference about the student's covert skill, namely, the ability to churn out narrative essays.

This is the mission of all kinds of classroom assessments; namely, to elicit evidence so that teachers can make accurate inferences about their students' unseen knowledge and skills. The teacher then uses these inferences to make instructional decisions for her students who, because of classroom assessment, are now better understood.

Although many classroom assessments are, in fact, the paper-and-pencil tests that most of us experienced when we ambled through school, today's assessments also include a variety of informal ways of collecting evidence about students' accomplishments. In the middle of a lesson, for instance, a teacher might ask students to answer a series of multiple-choice questions presented on the chalkboard or on an overhead screen. But instead of requiring students to write down their answers, the teacher might instead tell students to, "on the count of three," hold up a 5-by-8 inch card with a large A, B, C, D, or E on it. By quickly scanning students' cards, the teacher can discern how well they appear to be mastering what's being taught. Similar assessment strategies could be used for true-false items, whereby students would hold up cards containing a T, F, or question mark (to signify uncertainty). No grades need be involved in assessments that occur as part of the instructional process.

Other less traditional forms of classroom assessment might include small groups of students quizzing one another, sometimes using quizzes the teacher provides and sometimes constructing their own. This form of peer assessment is also intended to collect evidence so that inferences can be made about students' covert skills and knowledge.

Students can also be given self-assessment materials so that, using questions and answer keys constructed by the teachers, students can measure their own progress and determine how satisfactory their performance is. Self-assessments are being used in school more frequently nowadays than in years past.

In other words, while classroom assessment can certainly consist of the typical tests we have used for decades—written exams consisting of multiple-choice questions, short-answer items, or essays—today's conception of assessment embraces a wider array of techniques. Almost any procedure that elicits evidence that can be use to make reasonable inferences about students' unseen skills or knowledge can be considered a legitimate classroom assessment tactic.

Tests as tools to determine grades

Historically, teachers have used tests to help them grade their students. This time-honored use of classroom assessments meshes nicely with a traditional view of teaching in which the teacher's task is to get students to learn certain things. The teacher then tests those students to see how well they did, in fact, learn what they were supposed to. If students' performance on a test signifies mastery of what the teacher taught, then they are typically rewarded with high grades. If students garner enough high grades on enough tests, then the teacher gives them a high grade for the entire course or, for elementary students, for a particular subject, such as social studies or math.

Because most of today's adults went through school at a time when the dominant purpose of classroom testing was to help teachers grade their students, a prevalent perception among both educators and noneducators is that the chief mission of classroom testing is to help teachers determine students' grades.

Some classroom tests, of course, yield numerical scores rather than letter grades. For example, suppose a sixth-grade teacher, Mr. Johnson, gives a spelling exam in which he reads aloud twenty words from a list of 250 "spelling devils." Students write out each word, and they then correct each others' exams as Mr. Johnson reads aloud the correct spellings. Students' scores can range from zero to twenty, and the tests are returned to students with an indication of number correct rather than a letter grade. If the teacher wishes to assign letter grades, of course, the teacher must decide how many correct answers are needed in order for a student to be given an A, a B, and so on.

Whether classroom assessments are given letter grades or numerical scores, the overriding purpose of almost all teacher-constructed classroom tests is to grade students. Teachers understand this, as do students.

Tests as motivation mechanisms

A second purpose of classroom assessment, which flows directly from determining grades, is to motivate students to study with more energy. Because most students want to earn good grades and because they know they are apt to perform better on tests if they have prepared properly, many teachers use tests to motivate—that is, to spur their students to make a greater effort.

How many times, for example, have you heard students planning "cram sessions" so they can ready themselves for an important exam? Most teachers are shrewd enough to realize that the prospect of an exam that is key in determining grades can energize students' study efforts. And, of course, because the mission of all teachers is to get their students to learn, the use of test as motivating devices makes sense. The more important an upcoming exam is, the more effort students are apt to put into preparing for it, which teachers hope will lead to loads of lasting learning for their students.

An admission

Lest you think that I am above using classroom tests to grade students or spur them to greater effort, I freely admit that during most of my teaching career I was right in there with the rest of my colleagues, grading and motivating up a storm with my classroom tests. I thought, as did my fellow teachers, that this was the proper role for classroom assessments. It was the way our own teachers had used tests on us and, most significantly, we'd never been told that there was any other role for assessments. In short, I (we) didn't know any better.

So, please realize that I am not sniping at teachers who still exclusively use their classroom assessments to help grade their students or to stimulate intensified studying. I've been there, and I've done more than my share of precisely that. I can still recall the hundreds of grade books in which I dutifully recorded thousands of test grades and then assigned the overall grade for each student. I can also recall many times when I unashamedly used the importance of an upcoming test in determining grades as a blatant ploy to encourage my students to study with flat-out fervor.

If there is any sin associated with these typical uses of classroom assessments, then I can take my place near the head of the sinners' parade. But, as is true with most teachers, I simply didn't know I was doing anything wrong. That's usually the problem with errors of omission; those doing the omitting rarely recognize that they're failing to do what they ought to be doing. Let's turn, then, to what's so wrong about only using classroom assessments in a traditional manner.

Mistake number two: failing to use classroom assessments formatively

When teachers only use classroom assessment in a traditional manner, they fail to capitalize on a dividend of assessments that can have huge educational payoffs for students. A substantial body of evidence now exists to demonstrate convincingly that when classroom measurement is employed as part of the formative assessment process, students benefit big time. And there it is, the second of the six stumbling blocks preventing schools' success: teachers' relying on classroom assessments only to grade or motivate students rather than as part of the formative assessment process.

We now have compelling research that attests to the payoffs of using classroom assessments formatively. If teachers fail to use their assessments in this manner, students will be educationally shortchanged. What makes teachers' failure to use assessments formatively so serious is simply that they should know better. In fact, we should have known better for well over a decade.

FORMATIVE ASSESSMENT: A POTENT
BUT UNDERUSED PROCESS

Formative assessment defined

Let's start with a look at what formative assessment is (and what it isn't), and then consider the evidence supporting its value. In recent years, we have witnessed a bit of a brouhaha about the definition of formative assessment. I've attended a number of education conferences in which speakers have, in my view, played fairly fast and loose as they laid out what they think it is. As a consequence of these sometimes conflicting definitions, more than a few teachers and administrators have become understandably confused about the nature of formative assessment.

Not long ago, I wrote a book about formative assessment,[1] and out of either authorial loyalty or simple stubbornness, I think the definition I used in that volume is altogether serviceable. Here it is:

> Formative assessment is a planned process in which assessment-elicited evidence of students' status is used by teachers to adjust their ongoing instructional procedures or by students to adjust their current learning tactics.

Note that formative assessment is a process, and a planned process at that. It's a process that uses assessment-elicited evidence for teachers to adjust their instruction or for students to adjust their learning tactics. (By *learning tactics* I mean the procedures a student is using, such as study techniques, to master the material being taught.) As you can see from the definition above, formative assessment is most assuredly not a test. Moreover, there is no such thing as a "formative test." Tests are used *during* the formative assessment *process*, but tests are not, in themselves, formative assessments. Rather, tests are the evidence-gathering tools we use while the formative assessment process takes place.

Formative assessment can be contrasted with summative assessment, in which a more final determination is made about the effectiveness of instruction or about students' mastery of a body of material. Thus, when state officials require students to complete standardized accountability tests each year as a way of evaluating the instructional success of the state's schools, these tests are clearly being used *summatively*. The instructional activity whose effects are being measured has already been completed. Similarly, when teachers use classroom tests to help them decide on grades for their students, those tests are also being used summatively; the student's grade is being doled out for an already completed effort.

Tests that are employed formatively, however, help determine whether immediate adjustments are called for in classroom instruction. The core of formative assessment is an ongoing process wherein teachers and/or students use evidence elicited by assessment to adjust (if necessary) what they're doing in the classroom.

In a typical classroom where the teacher is using formative assessment, you'd see a wide range of both formal and informal assessment approaches (such as brief quizzes, self-testing, and peer assessment). The results of those assessments would not be used to grade students but to help teachers decide whether to adjust their instruction or to help students decide whether to adjust how they are trying to learn. These assessment results, therefore, are being used to form teachers' future instructional practices and/or students' future learning tactics—hence the term formative. In a classroom where formative assessment is in full flower, you'll find both teachers and students monitoring the success of their efforts by using an assessment-based estimate to determine how much learning has taken place.

We've seen that formative assessment is a process, not a test. But there are also things that formative assessment is not. One thing it is not is a teacher's unplanned, serendipitous use of student cues to adjust instruction. Sensible teachers, surely since the time of Socrates, use students' reactions to help figure out whether explanations need to be altered. When Socrates delivered an explanation of some profound truth and Plato's face registered puzzlement, surely Socrates doubled back and explained his point more clearly. But formative assessment calls for reliance on carefully considered out assessment evidence—not on observations of students' facial expressions—to guide teacher's instructional adjustments. Formative assessment is a carefully planned process, not a spur-of-the-moment snaring of assessment evidence.

Another thing formative assessment *isn't* is what is generally referred to these days as *interim tests* (also called *benchmark tests*). Interim tests are administered every two or three months, typically by a school or school district, as a way of monitoring students' mastery of a set of targeted curricular aims. Often those aims turn out to be the knowledge or skills assessed in annual accountability tests, and based on these (typically standardized) interim tests, predictions can usually be made about which students are or are not likely to succeed on those tests. Interim tests are sometimes erroneously characterized as formative assessments by the companies that sell them. So far, however, there is no solid research evidence of such interim tests helping students learn what they

---

SIDEBAR 2.1

An Assessment-Free Classroom Adjustment

Not all sensible classroom adjustments are made on the basis of assessment evidence. In trying to recall real-world examples of teachers making shrewd instructional adjustments without assessment data, I decided that the most vivid example I ever saw took place in Ethiopia, about forty years ago. Near the end of a three-week visit to observe UCLA-trained Peace Corps volunteers in Ethiopia (see sidebar 1.2), I had finished looking in on the classes of several volunteers in Harar, a town in the eastern part of the country. As the school headmaster and I were walking down the hall of his school, I told him that I had observed American teachers in many parts of his country, but I had not yet watched an Ethiopian teacher instructing in Amharic, the chief language of that nation. I asked for an opportunity to do so.

He instantly obliged by taking me into an adjacent building where about thirty fourth-grade children were being taught, in Amharic, by a female Ethiopian teacher. Apparently a lesson in language arts was going on because there was an active dialogue taking place between the teacher and her students. After a few minutes, the headmaster whispered to me that he needed to attend to other matters in the office and asked if I would be all right on my own. I assured him I would, and remained standing near the door as he left. Although I could not understand the language being used, I was immensely impressed by the teacher's skill in getting so many students to be so actively involved in what she was teaching.

After another ten minutes of the language arts lesson, however, I heard thunder in the distance. At that moment, the teacher—who had apparently also heard the sounds of a distant storm—instantly switched from an oral activity to a silent mathematics lesson. The students retrieved bottle caps

need to learn. Some firms that peddle interim-testing systems tout their assessments as "research proven," but that's simply false. Moreover, because formative assessment calls for the gathering of evidence that can lead to immediate adjustments in teachers' instruction or students' learning tactics, then timely classroom assessment is almost always required. Interim assessments, because they are trying to serve a number of teachers whose curricular pacing varies, can rarely supply the evidence to help

from their desks and began using them to solve math problems the teacher had previously written on the chalkboard. I didn't know why she had made such a quick adjustment, but it certainly had not been based on assessment evidence. I soon had my answer.

A few minutes later, when rain began to beat down on the galvanized metal roof covering the classroom, the noise was downright deafening. Given that din, no other sounds, surely including an oral language arts lesson, could have been heard. The teacher was being proactive when she quickly switched gears from an oral to a silent activity. I was genuinely impressed. Clearly, this teacher's past experiences had shown her that the coming rain called for instructional alterations in what was going on in class. Soon, with thunder pealing loudly, the rain pounding down, and more than a few flashes of lightning, the lights in the classroom went out. I was not astounded by this, however, because Ethiopian electricity in those days was fairly unpredictable. Many of the children looked up at me and smiled. I returned their smiles, a bit indulgently, I suspect, and the lights soon went back on.

But after a few more minutes, the lights went out once more, and this apparent power outage was again followed by students smiling at the visitor, the visitor returning their smiles, and the lights once more coming on. Soon this sequence had occurred for the third time, and I found myself musing that there I was, a Los Angeles professor in rural Africa, hence I shouldn't be even mildly surprised by the lights-on-lights-off sequence I was observing.

At that point, however, the teacher walked over to where I was standing and, in perfect English, fairly shouted in my ear, "Excuse me, sir, but you keep leaning on the mercury light switch."

I realized then that it was not the indulgently smiling visitor who had figured out what was going on, but the indulgently smiling fourth graders. The big-city prof felt full-on foolish.

teachers or students make on-the-spot adjustments—or even to make adjustments for the immediate future.

I'm not trying to clobber the potential contributions of interim tests. If they don't take too much time to administer, and they're not too expensive, they might very well supply teachers with instructionally useful information. All I'm trying to point out is that at the moment there is no compelling research evidence supporting the instructional merits of interim testing. Moreover, when commercial vendors try to tout these tests by piggybacking them on the empirical evidence supporting formative assessment, they are playing fast and loose with the truth.

Levels of implementation

If you look back at the definition of formative assessment, you'll see that there are two sets of actors in this classroom drama, the teacher and the students. Moreover, if you think about the ways different teachers are apt to apply it, you'll realize that there is likely to be substantial diversity in the ways teachers "make friends with" formative assessment.

Because there are two sorts of players in formative assessments, it can be confusing to lump the functions of these two groups together. For instance, is it formative assessment when a teacher uses assessment evidence to adjust instruction but does not let students use this same evidence to adjust their learning tactics? Or is it better formative assessment if both the teacher and the students are using assessment data to monitor and alter (if needed) what they are up to? Because clarity can be compromised when we think of diverse versions of formative assessment as one big blob, I have been encouraging educators to employ the following four-level conceptualization of formative assessment:

- *Level 1: Teachers' Instructional Adjustments.* Teachers collect evidence they use to decide whether to adjust their current or immediately upcoming instruction as a way to improve the effectiveness of that instruction.

- *Level 2: Students' Learning Tactic Adjustments.* Students use evidence of the current status of their skills and knowledge to decide whether to adjust the procedures they're using in an effort to learn.

- *Level 3: Classroom Climate Shift.* Teachers apply formative assessment in a way that transforms a traditional, comparison-dominated classroom—where the main purpose of assessment is to assign grades—into an atypical, learning-dominated classroom where the main purpose of assessment is to improve the quality of teaching and learning.

- *Level 4: Schoolwide Implementation.* An entire school (or district) promotes teachers' use of one or more levels of formative assessment, chiefly through conventional professional development activities and teacher learning communities.

When formative assessment is sorted into these four levels, it is easier to discuss variations in this powerful process. Moreover, to use formative assessment authentically, a teacher does not need to incorporate all of the first three levels into his or her instructional practice. A teacher who only gets as far as Level 1 is still likely to help students learn more effectively than if no formative assessment had been used at all. Do I think there is virtue in installing all four levels in a school or district? Absolutely! But I'd rather have kids be on the receiving end only of Level 1 than to get no formative assessment at all. Most important, educators should not mush these quite distinctive flavors of formative assessment together as though they are one. Each deserves specific attention and requires different kinds of adjustments.

Let's turn now to the reasons that teachers' failure to employ formative assessment constitutes a serious error of omission. Logic alone tells us that it makes sense to determine whether a person needs to alter an ongoing activity by measuring the impact of that activity. And experience shows that when human beings try to achieve a given end, they generally evaluate the effectiveness of their means by finding out if the end was, in fact, achieved. That's clearly what's going on in formative assessment. It's just commonsensical. But we have more than common sense to tell us that formative assessment works. We have evidence!

Supportive evidence

If there were only conjecture and no empirical evidence to support using classroom assessment formatively, then it wouldn't be such a sin for teachers not to use formative assessment in their classrooms. But there is empirical evidence, and that's why teachers' failure to employ this proven process that benefits students is a serious error of omission. We've had this evidence on our pedagogical plates for more than a decade, and that's far too long not to be acting on it. Let me review the chief features of this evidence.

In the spring of 1998, a significant review of research on classroom assessment appeared in *Assessment in Education.* Authored by two British researchers, Paul Black and Dylan Wiliam, this carefully conducted analysis of ten years worth of published research on classroom assessment arrived at a set of conclusions that, at the time, many educators regarded as quite startling.[2] Let me summarize briefly how these two researchers went about their work.

They began by using two earlier review articles as the baseline for their review,[3] and then tackled essentially all of the research dealing with classroom assessment that had been published in the previous ten years— roughly between 1988 and 1998. Black and Wiliam considered more than 680 published investigations, selecting about 250 of the most solid studies to scrutinize more carefully. Based on a thoughtful and well-described analytic review of these studies, the two concluded that "the research reported here shows conclusively that formative assessment does improve learning."[4] And what about the magnitude of this improvement in learning? Are we talking about something substantial or fairly trivial? Black and Wiliam contend that the gains in student learning triggered by formative assessment were "amongst the largest ever reported for educational interventions." So, to summarize, Black and Wiliam's persuasive review of a full decade's worth of empirical investigations reveals that the use of formative assessment leads to whopping gains in students learning.

Because Black and Wiliam's article appeared in a scholarly, refereed journal, some observers might conclude that the review simply could have escaped the attention of American educators. After all, far fewer people read *Assessment in Education* than, say, *USA Today* or the *Wall Street Journal.* However, about six months later, Black and Wiliam published an article in the *Phi Delta Kappan,* a far more accessible and widely read journal.[5] In the second article, the two Brits summarized their earlier, more lengthy review, again citing the substantial learning dividends obtainable by using classroom assessments formatively.

One of the judgments reached by Black and Wiliam that makes their conclusions so compelling is their view that formative assessment is remarkably robust; that is, when formative assessment is implemented by teachers, it is almost certain to work. The two point out: "Significant gains can be achieved by many different routes, and initiatives here are not likely to fail through neglect of delicate and subtle features."[6] In their review, Black and Wiliam supply many examples of research studies in which it is apparent that formative assessment makes a contribution to students' learning. As they point out:

> However, the consistent feature across the variety of these examples is that they all show that attention to formative assessment can lead to significant learning gains. Although there is no guarantee that it will do so irrespective of the context and the particular approach adopted, we have not come across any report of negative effects following on an enhancement of formative practice.[7]

The 1998 research review by Black and Wiliam laid a potent pedagogical truth smack in the middle of American educators' laps: If teachers use formative assessment in their classes, kids will clearly benefit. If teachers fail to adopt this use of classroom assessment, however, it indeed constitutes a significant error of omission.

FORMATIVE ASSESSMENT: TWO INNARDS ONLY

"Innards" is a term that originated in the early nineteenth century and, as my dictionary tells the tale, is a distortion of local dialect, "inwards" referring to the internal parts of a body or a mechanism. It is a plural noun to be sure, and I've never seen it used in the singular, "innard." However, I don't really want to engage in a full-fledged analysis of formative assessment's many innards, thus I offer a terse treatment of only two. I think it's important to understand both of these points in order to gain a more accurate understanding of why, when teachers fail to use formative assessment in their classrooms, they are cheating their students instructionally.

Learning progressions as precursors

Let's get underway with a look at Innard Number One. Remember, formative assessment is a planned process in which assessment evidence is collected so teachers and/or students can alter what they are doing. Well, if such evidence is to be gathered in a thoughtful manner during the instructional process, precisely when should such ongoing assessments take place? The answer lies in a teacher's use of learning progressions.

A learning progression is a sequenced set of building blocks (subskills and/or bodies of enabling knowledge) that lead to the mastery of a more remote curricular aim. Sometimes referred to as "task analyses," learning progressions simply represent the things we believe students need to learn along the way in order to achieving the ultimate curricular aim. For example, if the target curricular aim is the ability to analyze complex political conflicts, the relevant subskills might include the ability to distinguish points of view expressed by participants on opposing sides, while bodies of enabling knowledge might include factual information about the history of the conflict.

Figure 2.1 illustrates a learning progression containing four building blocks—two subskills and two bodies of enabling knowledge. The building blocks are arranged in the sequence in which the student is expected to master them. As you can see, the person who constructed this learning progression thinks that in order to successfully master Target Curriculum Aim X, a student must first master Enabling Knowledge A, then Subskill A, then Enabling Knowledge B, and then Subskill B. For example, if the target curricular aim had called for students to be able to incorporate appropriate punctuation in their written compositions, then we might find one body of enabling knowledge (Enabling Knowledge A) setting forth a series of comma-usage rules and the next building block in the learning progression (Subskill A) requiring students to be able to apply those rules in their own writing. Similarly, Enabling Knowledge B might lay out other punctuation rules and Subskill B might call for the application of those rules.

Learning progressions, because they require serious thinking from those who design them, are typically reserved for the pursuit of significant target curricular aims—for example, an important cognitive skill in a math class that might take several weeks to teach, or a sophisticated science skill that might involve two months of instruction. And because learning progressions can easily become quite complicated, it is sensible to focus only on the identification of building blocks that are absolutely

FIGURE 2.1   *An Illustrative Learning Progression*

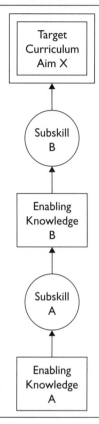

necessary for students to master if they are to achieve the target curricular aim.

The building blocks of a well-designed learning progression should be
seen as "must learn" commodities. If students are to master a targeted
curricular aim, they must learn each of the subskills and bodies of
enabling knowledge in the learning progression. Accordingly, to make
sure that those building blocks have been mastered by students, a
teacher needs to collect assessment-elicited evidence regarding each of
those building blocks. Only then will teachers know whether to adjust
their instruction as it relates to a particular building block. Only then
will students know whether to adjust the learning tactics they are using

when trying to master a particular building block. This is why learning progressions are regarded as so necessary to carry out formative assessment successfully.

As indicated previously, the assessments need not be formal paper-and-pencil tests—on the contrary, a whole range of informal assessment procedures might be used. But the central notion is that formative assessment cannot work well unless plans are made and implemented to collect evidence regarding students' mastery of each key building block in the learning progression that leads to the achievement of a more terminal curricular aim.

But, as indicated above, learning progressions are not only time-consuming to create, they require loads of first-rate thinking from those who construct them. Moreover, they can easily become far more complicated than they ought to be or need to be. And this leads me to the second important "innard" of formative assessment.

Right-size bites rule

Formative assessment works. It works even when teachers use it in different ways. When formative assessment works, kids end up learning more. Therefore, just as surely as school buses run late, it is certain that formative assessment should be used more widely than it currently is.

But this is the point at which I start to worry. Having spent more than a half-century as a teacher, I can guarantee that I've seen dozens of fine-sounding instructional ideas founder, chiefly because they turned out to be too much work—that is, they took too much time for teachers to implement. For example, a decade or so ago, many educators became entranced with the idea that portfolio assessment would provide a fairer, more accurate picture of students' achievement. There were supportive speeches given at education conferences and supportive books written by proponents of portfolio assessment. The gist of this approach was for teachers to collect evolving work samples from students over an extended period of time (perhaps an entire school year). During that time, the teacher would often sit down with students to evaluate their portfolios, chiefly to encourage them to become skilled in evaluating the ever-improving work samples that were being collected. When teachers used portfolios as part of their ongoing instruction, the reports were

almost always positive. However, when states tried to employ this measure in an accountability context, portfolio assessment definitely flopped.

These days, if you set out in search of teachers who are using portfolio
assessment as the backbone of their instructional strategy, you'll be doing
more searching than finding. The problem with portfolio assessment is
that it simply takes too much time for most teachers to stick with it for
more than a year or two. Classroom operations that take too much time
or too much effort are rarely destined to endure. This is a clear and present danger that advocates of formative assessment must be constantly on
guard to avoid. Educators dare not make formative assessment onerous,
because onerous formative assessment would surely become forgotten
formative assessment.

Thus, although there are countless innovative ways of assessing students, care must be taken to ensure that those assessments will actually
be used. And though it is possible to devise learning progressions with a
dozen or more building blocks, remember that the teacher needs to collect assessment evidence indicating how well students are doing with
respect to each of those blocks. A large pile of building blocks that must
be assessed will quickly dissuade most teachers from wanting to paddle
in the formative assessment pool.

If some teachers turn out to want more from formative assessment,
then there are four levels to choose from, as presented previously. But
formative assessment, *even if limited to Level 1,* benefits students. It will
be far better to see scads of Level 1 formative assessment in our classrooms on a continuing basis than to see multi-level formative assessment
in place only for a brief while. Right-sized bites of formative assessment
can be chewed and digested over the years. Too-big bites aren't the answer.

I hope it's clear that the second stumbling block to the success of our
schools is that a process that's demonstrably capable of helping students
become better educated is being underused. We have known for more
than a decade, chiefly due to the research syntheses of Black and Wiliam,
that this use of classroom assessment procedures will—in myriad variations—end up benefiting students.[8] Yet, in spite of this powerful evidence, most American educators continue to use classroom assessments
only to grade or motivate their students. The underutilization of classroom assessment—the failure to install the formative-assessment process

widely in our schools—constitutes a significant and harmful error of omission.

A LESSON-LEARNT SOLUTION

Sticking with the British past tense for "learn," the lesson-learnt solution to this second problem is straightforward, yet definitely not as easy to pull off as it might initially appear. What we need to do is get more teachers to use one or more levels of formative assessment in their classrooms, but finding ways to go about it is, of course, where real-world difficulties scurry forward.

Let's face it, to persuade additional teachers to employ formative assessment, we need to have a substantial number of teachers—many of whom believe they are doing a satisfactory instructional job—admit that they may have been performing less effectively than they should. And once that difficult admission has been made, we must persuade hoards of those teachers not only to adopt a new way of thinking about the role of classroom assessment but to actually use the formative assessment process with their students. Pulling off this kind of substantial change in almost any professional person's conduct—educational or noneducational—represents a nontrivial task. It is far easier to *advocate* change than it is to *bring* change about. How, then, do we go about getting large numbers of teachers to use formative assessment?

Well, as a starting point, we must remember that teachers, like other human beings, want to be good at what they do. When people are skilled at what they do, whether they're plumbers or astronauts, they typically feel good about themselves—that is, their skill mastery induces a solid dose of self-esteem. In fact, the quest for self-esteem is a potent motivator for almost all of us. The challenge for those who want to promote the widespread use of formative assessment, therefore, is to convince teachers that when they employ the process in their classrooms, they will not only become more instructionally competent, they will *be seen* as having become more instructionally competent. Moreover, they'll be helping their students learn more effectively. If teachers can enhance their own self-esteem—their perceived effectiveness—and also benefit their students, those are three pretty potent motivators. At bottom, a solution strategy to promote formative assessment needs to be based on these three pay-offs for teachers.

Common colds and formative assessment

I've spent a good many hours thinking about how to entice more teachers to hop aboard the formative assessment flotilla. Even so, I'm far from certain that I have the most sensible solution-strategy to propose. Nevertheless, I want to describe what I've concluded might work. It's a two-step strategy, and it parallels what might happen if we were suddenly to discover a cure for the common cold.

For the sake of this explanation, please assume for a moment that scientists have stumbled upon a cure for the common cold. The cure consists of a single, low-cost capsule which, when ingested, makes all cold symptoms disappear. For adults, the cold symptoms vanish in less than four hours and, for small children, all symptoms disappear in less than two hours. With good reason, this medicinal breakthrough is widely hailed as a medical miracle.

Well, as soon as federal approval for the new drug has been secured, wouldn't you expect that people in all walks of life would be talking about this miracle drug? The media would be crammed with stories about the cold-cure capsule. Don't you think most physicians would be prescribing this new cure with gusto? And what about the parents of small children? Wouldn't we find parents clamoring for the new cure so they could offer relief when their children came down with a cold? Any parent who has had to cope with a child's cough, sore throat, or runny nose would surely be lining up to secure the new capsules.

To get this new cold cure to do its magic widely, it would be necessary first to let the world know that there was such a cure, and then to make the cold capsules available to anyone who had a cold and wanted to get rid of it.

Well, although formative assessment may not have the glamour of a cure for the common cold, it shares some striking similarities with our make-believe capsule. First off, it works! Second, it works! And third, as you have guessed, it works! In this instance, "works" means that when teachers use formative assessment, children learn better. In the world of education, a surefire way to help kids learn better is remarkably close to a medical cure for the common cold.

If the medical profession were to allow an affordable, proven cure for the common cold to languish, there would be a public outrage, especially from parents—and there should be! Yet, if the education profession lets an affordable, proven way to better educate kids languish, shouldn't there be a similar display of outrage from the public, and especially from parents? Well, I sure think there should be. And, of course, the more widespread the outrage, the more likely it would be that action would be triggered. Squeaky wheels and squeaky parents typically get attention.

Yet, if most educators are not even familiar with the fundamentals of formative assessment, as is currently the case, and if most parents of school-age children have never even heard of formative assessment, as is currently the case, there is little likelihood of seeing any outrage from either parents or educators. Even if the potential payoffs of formative assessment are widely recognized, however, we still need mechanisms to help teachers actually use formative assessment. These conditions, then, underlie the two-step strategy for dramatically increasing the use of formative assessment that I'll now describe. Its two stages, put simply, are getting the word out and providing options for implementation. Let's look briefly at what's involved in both of these steps.

Getting the word out

To get under way, those who want to see formative assessment more widely used must devote energy to getting the message out—that is, to let educators, parents, and policymakers know that formative assessment is a research-proven process that helps students become better educated. The message can be succinct or it can be effusive, but the first step in my strategy is simply to get the word out. Only when abundant numbers of educators, education policymakers, and parents grasp the reality that we have a potent way of helping kids learn more effectively but aren't using it can we ever hope to see more teachers employ formative assessment.

For instance, the Council of Chief State School Officers (CCSSO) has taken a leadership role in disseminating information about formative assessment. The CCSSO is, in the United States, the organization of state superintendents of each state's public schools. Sometimes referred to as commissioners or secretaries, these individuals, whether elected or appointed, obviously occupy influential positions in their states. Consequently, CCSSO is also an influential organization on a national scale in the U.S.

In 2006, CCSSO officials recognized the enormous potential of formative assessment to boost the quality of students' learning. CCSSO then established a standing advisory committee to offer recommendations to the organization's leaders regarding how to best promote greater acceptance of formative assessment in the nation's public schools. One recommendation was to shift the focus of the CCSSO's longstanding (and well attended) national conference on large-scale assessment to a more balanced view that also featured classroom formative assessment. In 2008, the CCSSO National Conference on Student Assessment did, in fact, give substantial attention to formative assessment. At the same time, CCSSO created a collaborative of about twenty states whose department of education personnel had registered interest in the formative assessment process. Several states, including Iowa, have made substantial commitments to having their state's educators become more conversant with the nature of formative assessment. Clearly, CCSSO has committed itself to furthering interest in, and use of, formative assessment.

The CCSSO story could obviously be replicated in other associations—associations of teachers and educational administrators, school boards, or other education advocacy groups. If we really want to get this formative assessment process into the hands of the teachers who should be dispensing it to children and satisfying parents, we need to persuade more policymakers and association leaders that this is a mission their organizations should adopt.

Step one, then, is getting the word out. It can be done individually or organizationally and, if possible, in both ways. Let's turn now to step two.

Providing implementation options

Formative assessment can be installed by teachers, one at a time, all by themselves. However, solitary implementation is much less likely to succeed than approaches that involve multiple teachers in an extended-duration activity with other teachers. This kind of support system can, over time, alter even the most ingrained teacher behaviors.

Remember, formative assessment is a process, a process wherein teachers plan carefully when and how to collect assessment evidence, then figure out whether this evidence dictates an adjustment in (1) the teachers' instruction or (2) the learning tactics students are employing. It is a process that has plenty of parts—some of them moving. It is a process that takes time to figure out and refine. It is a process that is more apt to be successful when groups of educators have an opportunity to collaboratively sharpen that process over time.

It would the height of folly for a school administrator to deliver a rousing speech in support of formative assessment at the beginning of a school year and then hope that most of the school's teachers would, on their own, instantly put first-rate formative assessment into operation in their classrooms. That's simply not how the real-world of schooling works. If teachers are going to give formative assessment a serious whirl, they need collegial support.

A teacher who is attempting to make formative assessment work will face all sorts of questions. For example, what sorts of assessments should be used to efficiently measure students' current levels of achievement? And when assessment evidence has been collected and analyzed, what level of performance will indicate that a teacher's instruction should be altered? Finally, if adjustments are to be made, what sort are apt to be most effective?

If it is true that many hands make light work, it is equally true that many heads make formative assessment fly. And this is why many proponents of formative assessment urge that it be implemented in the context of a *learning community*—some group of like-minded individuals who meet over an extended period to share insights on how to use formative assessment most effectively. If these working groups involve only teachers, they are typically referred to as *teacher learning communities*. If both teachers and administrators participate, the groups are usually labeled *professional learning communities*.

For several years, Dylan Wiliam—the researcher who, with Paul Black, spurred great interest in formative assessment back in 1998 with their compelling review of classroom assessment research—worked at Educational Testing Service (ETS) in Princeton, New Jersey. While there (or, as Dylan would put it, *whilst* there), he and his ETS colleagues developed, tried out, and refined a systematic model for getting teachers to employ formative assessment. That approach, called Keeping Learning on Track (KLT), is an example of an implementation strategy rooted in teacher learning communities. Groups of, say, eight to ten teachers meet weekly, biweekly, or monthly during a school year to address a variety of issues and procedural choices associated with the installation of formative assessment in participating teachers' classrooms. Early tryouts of the KLT program are well described in an ETS research report.[9] The heart of the implementation program is the systematic consideration of the most important choices faced by teachers who want to play the formative assessment game appropriately. By meeting every few weeks, doing at least some work between meetings, and continuing to meet for a substantial period of time, members of these teacher learning communities almost always develop genuine conversance with the main features, as well as the nuances, of the formative assessment process.

During the last few years, as I have visited with many teachers and administrators about their use of formative assessment, the continuing complaint I hear is that teachers are given too little time to organize meaningful teacher learning communities or professional learning communities. Remember, it does not take an enormous amount of money to get one of these learning communities under way. All that's needed is a handful of participants and some low-cost reading materials on formative assessment procedures. Formative assessment as an instructional intervention is wonderfully affordable, but it can't work if teachers are not given time to enhance their professional prowess.

Let's say, for instance, that a school principal is eager to get his teachers to adopt formative assessment in their classrooms. If that principal can set aside, say, two hours every other week for teacher learning communities to meet as they work to become more proficient in using formative assessment to benefit their students, then there is every reason to believe that this low-cost professional development will, in time, help many teachers become more adroit at using the formative-assessment process. However, without a commitment of sufficient time for professional development, widespread implementation of formative assessment is apt to be feckless. Surely, it would be great to have a series of learning communities kicked off by bringing in an outside specialist for a few workshop sessions. But such workshops directed by outside specialists are not absolutely necessary. What is absolutely necessary is sufficient *time* for learning communities to function properly. Allocated time, not wishing, will make formative assessment flourish.

CHAPTER THREE

A Preoccupation with Instructional Process

A third impediment to the success of our schools stems from an especially common mistake—paying attention to the wrong things. When we pay attention to the wrong things, we can't pay attention to the right things. Unfortunately, in the world of education, we find too many teachers paying attention to the instructional procedures they use, rather than to what happens to their students as a result of those procedures. Simply put, too many teachers are preoccupied with instructional process. And they're focusing on the wrong thing.

Teachers' preoccupation with instructional process is one of the more serious mistakes I've seen educators make, and I've see it made for more than a half-century. Thinking back on my years as a high school teacher, I definitely made this particular mistake myself—probably on a daily or even hourly basis. As a rookie teacher, I was almost completely focused on what I would be doing in class, on the sorts of activities I would provide for my students. My all-consuming dread was that I would run out of things to do. I feared that my lesson plan for a particular class would take markedly less time than time I had foreseen: There I would be, looking at a roomful of students with twenty minutes remaining in the period and with nothing to do that remotely resembled teaching. I would be exposed for the fraud that I was. I even had nightmares about running out of instructional activities in my classes.

During my stint as a novice high school teacher, I rarely thought about what the effects of the instructional activities I had chosen would be. Come to think of it, I doubt if I ever *seriously* thought about the effects of my instruction on my students. Instead, I was preoccupied with what was going to take place in class.

I'm not suggesting that most teachers are as obsessive as I was about running out of instructional activities, but I do suggest that many teachers make the same fundamental mistake I made back then, namely, being more concerned with instructional process than with instructional product. To be more explicit, I believe that most of today's teachers are more concerned with what goes on in class than with what happens to their students as a consequence of what goes on in class.

FOCUSING ON MEANS, NOT ENDS

The essence of this third unlearned lesson is that far too many educators—classroom teachers and those who supervise them—attend to instructional means rather than to the ends those means are supposed to bring about in students. Educators focused on means bring a general mindset to their work , thinking of instruction chiefly as what teachers do instead of what it helps students become. Over the long haul, this mentality will certainly diminish the quality of education we provide for our children. This sort of thinking, therefore, needs to be meaningfully modified.

Ends and means

Back in chapter 1, I drew a distinction between educational ends and educational means. Educational ends—that is, the knowledge, skills, and affect we want our students to acquire—were described as curricular aims. Educational means, in contrast, were seen as instruction—that is, the activities teachers provide in order to get their students to achieve the identified curricular aims. In short:

Curricular Aims = Educational Ends
Instruction = Educational Means

In all realms of life, people select particular means because they are thought most likely to accomplish whatever ends are sought. People go on diets, for example, because they want to lose weight. The diet is a person's chosen means to accomplish the desired end, weight loss.

Getting back to education, without exception teachers want their students to learn, and believe that what they do in their classrooms will help achieve that goal. But for many of them, the link between instructional procedures and their subsequent educational effects on students remains rather general and fuzzy. In fact, based on years of interacting with thousands of teachers, I submit that many teachers do not give serious thought to the way their instructional activities are supposed to impact their students' knowledge, skills, or affect.

If you could spend an hour or so in almost any faculty lounge in the nation and listen to what's being said about teaching, I'll wager a life's supply of dark-chocolate fudge sauce that almost all of the teaching talk you'd hear would be about instructional procedures, about what goes on in class. Oh, of course you'd also hear a fair amount of grousing about the need to prepare for state-level accountability tests, but when the conversation turned to what was actually happening in the classroom, odds are that the talk would be about instructional process. Rarely would you hear those teachers considering whether the instructional procedures they were discussing had actually worked. Many teachers, unfortunately, tend to judge the merits of their instructional procedures by how well they believe those procedures have been carried out.

And it's not just teachers whose eyes seem to be riveted on means rather than ends. Through the years, I've spoken to numerous principals and assistant principals regarding the strategies and tactics they employ to supervise and evaluate the teachers in their schools. Many of those administrators place great stock in being able to observe a teacher "in action." This is because many school administrators are convinced they can arrive at an accurate judgment about a teacher's instructional effectiveness based on their observations. School-site administrators, too, tend to be preoccupied with instructional process rather than with the consequences of that process.

Perils of preoccupation with process

What's so terrible about having educators focus on means rather than ends? Isn't it a good thing to have teachers give serious attention to the instructional activities that take place in their classes? Let me try to answer these two important questions.

A pair of negative consequences typically arise when teachers are excessively attentive to instructional procedures and give short shrift to whether curricular aims have been attained. First off, when teachers devote insufficient thought to how they'll determine whether their curricular aims have been achieved, there's a high likelihood that their instructional procedures will be off target—that is, they will not help students attain the desired ends. It should be apparent that when teachers have only a murky idea about the knowledge, skills, and/or affect their students are supposed to achieve, then those murk-masked ends won't be useful in guiding teachers to select instructional activities most likely to promote students' attainment of poorly understood curricular aims. The more clearly teachers understand where they're heading, the more likely it is they will get there. By not attending sufficiently to the nature of curricular ends, teachers will be more likely to select off-target instructional means.

A second adverse consequence of teachers' preoccupation with process is that such teachers tend to evaluate their own performance based on the quality of the instructional process they are using, not the payoff it produces. They fail to recognize that instructional procedures ought to be evaluated chiefly on the basis of whether they are successful in promoting student learning.

So, we see that teachers who are process preoccupied often employ off-target instructional activities because they are not clear about the curricular ends they are pursuing, and they often fail to evaluate their instructional procedures in the most appropriate way, namely, determining whether students mastered the desired curricular aims. The combined impact of these two difficulties is that kids are not taught as well as they should be—and that's what so terrible about having educators focus excessive attention on means rather than ends.

Different strokes

After a major football game, have you ever watched postgame interviews with players who took part in the game? Members of the losing team often say such things as, "We had a better passing attack" or "Our defense was superior to theirs." But if a TV interviewer, clearly trying to foment controversy, relays one of these "we-played-better" comments to members of the winning team, a one-word rejoinder from the victorious players always wins: "Scoreboard!"

The "scoreboard" response succinctly tells the world that, despite a losing player's claim that his team had a stronger this or a better that, the final score emphatically says—postgame rationalizations notwithstanding—the better team won. In other words, whatever the losing team's alleged superiority with respect to running, passing, or kicking, by the end of the game the winning team scored more points. Ends always trump means.

Football games, upon closer inspection, have more in common with what goes on in classrooms than merely the use of time-outs. In football, it's the final score—the end—that determines which team won the game. In the classroom, it's what students learn that determines whether the teacher's instruction worked. It's not the lucidity of the teacher's explanations, the spontaneity of classroom discussions, or the diligence with which students complete their homework. In short, it's not the quality of the instructional means that establish the success or failure of a teacher's instruction, it's what students learn—the ends—that matter.

One key reason we can't rely on classroom procedures to ascertain the quality of instruction is that in teaching there are definitely different strokes for different folks. Markedly different ways of teaching can work equally well. Teaching is a form of profound particularism—that is, in each instructional situation there is a particular teacher who will most surely possess a particular personality, particular pedagogical strengths or weaknesses, and particular ways of interacting with students. Then, too, there is the setting in which the instruction takes place, namely, a particular school building whose particular staff is guided by a particular principal. And, of course, there are always particular students being taught, each of whom arrives in class with a particular set of background experiences and a particular way they will learn most effectively. Teaching most surely takes place amid a profusion of particulars.

All this particularism translates into a simple but significant truth: we can't tell definitively whether a specific instructional procedure is going to work well. Oh, competent teachers will choose instructional procedures that, based on empirical research or a teacher's own experience, are likely to work well. But just as the proof of the pudding is revealed not by the pudding's ingredients but after the pudding has been eaten, the proof of instructional quality is revealed by what happens to students after they have experienced the instruction.

SIDEBAR 3.1
Particulars, Particulars

I've been a teacher for more than fifty years. Since retiring from UCLA about fifteen years ago, most of my teaching has been carried out in workshop settings or in short courses. But, whether teaching in high school, college, or out on the road, one thing I have learned for sure is that instructional situations differ—often dramatically. An instructional tactic that might work wonderfully in one setting might very well flop in another. Teaching procedures that fit one instructor beautifully might backfire when used by someone else. It's the same way with students—an instructional approach that might soar for one set of students could sink when used with another group. Any seasoned teacher realizes that instruction is a particularized enterprise. And, because I have had a half-century's worth of seasoning, my own teaching history is littered with examples of how a set of changed circumstances had a whopping effect on my instruction.

One of the most vivid examples of this in my own experience took place during my first college teaching job—at Kansas State College of Pittsburg, Kansas. Several years earlier, during my doctoral studies at Indiana University, my focus had been exclusively on instruction. I never took a course dealing with assessment because all I really wanted to do was teach prospective teachers how to instruct their students. One of the most thought-provoking books about teaching I read during my graduate studies was a book by Nathaniel Cantor called *The Dynamics of Learning*.[1] I actually read the book twice.

Cantor contended that the only kind of learning that really stuck—where students really internalized and used what they had learned—was learning they accomplished on their own. He recommended, therefore, an approach to instruction that was exceedingly nondirective in which the instructor deliberately and openly shifted the responsibility for learning from the teacher to the students. I was completely captivated by Cantor's argument and, after finishing my doctoral program, I vowed to try out his approach as soon as I could.

That opportunity came up for me during my first year of college teaching as a brand new assistant professor. The course I chose was Fundamentals of Curriculum, in which about twenty masters' degree candidates had enrolled. I tried to follow Cantor's advice closely, regarding *The Dynamics of Learning* as a sort of behind-the-scene scripture. I tried hard to set up the class as Cantor had suggested—that is, I told the students that there would be weekly assigned readings in a then-popular textbook about curriculum, and that they were to turn in a paper before each week's class regarding their reactions to the chapter assigned for the week. (We met once per week for four hours.) The class was to be conducted, however, as a series of student-led discussions. There would be no lectures from me, and I would not answer students' questions. I told the class that the entire responsibility for learning would be theirs, not mine.

Well, just as Cantor had predicted, after a few sessions in which I declined to answer students' questions and allowed periods of silence during discussions, students began to get visibly angry with me. During our fourth class session, one student asked me whether, when I accepted my monthly salary check: "Does your hand tremble? Aren't *you* supposed to be teaching us?"

But just as Cantor had prophesied, at about that time, most of the students finally realized that if they were going to learn about curriculum, they had better get cracking. The weekly discussions became intense and far more thoughtful. Students worked with each other and did, without question, assume complete responsibility for what they were to learn. What they learned they learned deeply and well. I was delighted, and looked back at the course as one of my finest instructional efforts.

So, when the next school year rolled around, I used Cantor's nondirective approach once more in the same curriculum course and with about the same number of master's degree students. During my first year's use of this instructional approach, I had learned a great deal about how to bounce students' questions back at them and deal (at least in my own head) with periods of silence during the discussions that sometimes lasted for several minutes. If anything, I was sure I would be more skilled at implementing Cantor's vision of teaching when I used it for a second group of students.

However, whereas the first year's class had been uncomfortable with periods of silence, the second year's class reveled in that silence. After a few class sessions, in fact, several students urged their classmates to "go for new records"

continued

SIDEBAR 3.1 *continued*

of silence. Although the first year's students had finally assumed responsibility for their own learning, the second year's students just didn't seem to care.

Finally, at mid-semester, I apologized to the students for what had been truly miserable instruction. I reverted to a traditional lecture approach, did what I could in the remaining class sessions, and regarded the whole endeavor as an unqualified disaster.

It was my view then, and still is, that the chief difference in the success of my two dips into Cantorian teaching was the students. Initially I had a group that included a number of students who were willing to take responsibility for their own learning. The rest of the class followed suit, and Cantor's approach purred. In my second bite of the nondirective apple, however, there was not one student who was willing to be responsible for what was to be learned. Put simply, an instructional approach that had worked well with a particular group of students had, with another group, fallen firmly on its fanny.

Teaching involves adjusting to the pile of particulars in which it takes place. You can't come up with an inflexible, one-size-fits-all approach to instruction. This is why teachers who worship instructional process and forget about the importance of product are destined for an almost certain comeuppance.

A series of instructional procedures—that might work wonderfully for Teacher X in Setting Y with Students Z—might prove to be disastrous when used by a different teacher in a different setting with different students. And this is why, because the goal of teachers should be to bring about worthwhile changes in students, not simply carry out instructional procedures, teachers must always be looking toward the impact of their instructional procedures on students. Teachers should, therefore, be focusing almost constantly on ends, not means. Teachers who are preoccupied with instructional process tend to miss out on two key contributions that a focus on curricular aims will yield. Let's look at both of those contributions.

TWO KEY CONTRIBUTIONS OF CURRICULAR AIMS

As noted earlier, the ends teachers hope their students will achieve are typically set forth as curricular aims. They are also labeled goals, objectives, content standards, expectancies, outcomes, targets, or some similar descriptor. Curricular aims describe the knowledge, skills, or affect (such as students' attitudes and interests) teachers are trying to get their students to acquire. Giving serious attention to curricular aims can make two major contributions to the quality of teachers' instructional efforts.

First, properly understood curricular aims can substantially advantage teachers as they design their instructional activities. This is just common sense. The better a person understands a desired end, the more likely it is that the person can adopt suitable means to accomplish that end. The more clearly a teacher understands the curricular ends students should be achieving, the more it is likely they will employ instructional procedures that can get students to achieve those aims. For teachers planning an instructional sequence, few factors are more beneficial than clarity of instructional intent. Properly understood curricular aims can help provide such clarity.

SIDEBAR 3.2

Advances in Accreditation Land

More than fifty years ago, as I began my doctoral studies at Indiana University, one of my first classes called for all students to complete a semester-long term project involving the application of a set of school-accreditation criteria to a real or fictitious elementary or secondary school. We were allowed to choose the accreditation framework we wished to employ in carrying out the assignment, and I selected the accreditation approach then used by the North Central Association (NCA) because at that time it was the chief accrediting agency for schools in the Midwest.

Only a few months earlier, I had been a high school teacher in a small eastern Oregon community, so I decided to use Heppner High School where I had taught as a focus for my class project, that is, application of the NCA accreditation criteria. Our assignment was to determine whether, using the accreditation approach we had chosen, the school being evaluated would have actually been accredited.

As a newcomer to the world of doctoral studies I was eager to do a solid job with this assignment, so I got under way immediately. What I discovered was that the thrust of the NCA accreditation criteria at that time were decidedly process focused. That is, those criteria dealt almost exclusively with such

continued

SIDEBAR 3.2 *continued*

process variables as the degrees a school's teachers had earned, the number of books in the school's library, the nature of the available audiovisual equipment, and the number of instructional days provided each year. There was fundamentally no attention given to any evidence of what students had actually learned.

You may think I was dismayed by this focus on process and the resultant inattention to the effects of instruction—but I wasn't. Remember, I was a novice in the doctoral studies game, and I figured that if a big outfit like NCA had decided to judge school quality using those process-focused evaluative factors, there must have been a good reason for it.

Because I was so motivated to succeed, I finished my report really early, after only a few weeks, and turned it in well before mid-term. My analysis indicated that Heppner High School would have been accredited using NCA criteria, but just barely.

What I didn't foresee, however, is that only one week later our professor spent almost ninety minutes reading aloud to our class (of about fifty students) substantial segments of my report. Fortunately, he did not identify the report as mine, but he often referred to Heppner High School as he used lengthy excerpts from my report as discussion triggers for well over an hour. When the class session was halfway finished, he gave us our usual 15-minute break, and as I listened to other students talking in the hallway, more than a few of them were annoyed with someone's early submission, saying essentially the same thing, namely, "Where in the hell is Heppner High School?"

Although I was a novice grad student, I was sensible enough not to reveal, that night or ever, I was the culprit in the premature term-paper submission.

So, back then, accreditation associations were totally caught up in the use of process variables. I've been pleased to note that during the subsequent fifty years, potent shifts have been seen in the approaches used by accreditation associations when they judge the quality of schools. For example, one of the nation's currently most influential accreditation associations, AdvanceED, now features evaluative criteria that are patently focused on what happens to students as a consequence of the instruction they receive. For instance, evidence is sought from assessment approaches that can be used to make defensible judgments about whether students have learned the things they were supposed to learn. Accreditation of schooling has moved meaningfully toward product instead of merely process.

A second contribution of curricular aims is that they provide a proper focus for assessing the effectiveness of instruction. That is, curricular aims should be the most salient factor in determining how successfully a teacher has taught. But, of course, evaluating a teacher's instructional success is one of the most difficult tasks facing those who lead our schools.

Let's consider, then, how teachers' attention to curricular ends can lead to both of these payoffs, better instructional design and better evaluation of teachers.

Designing instruction

For most educators, the holy trinity of their profession revolves around curriculum, instruction, and assessment. Curriculum, as noted before, refers to the knowledge and skills teachers want their students to acquire. Instruction describes the activities teachers ask their students to engage in as the desired aims are pursued. Included in instruction are such things as teachers' explanations, assigned reading, practice exercises, independent study, and how students complete homework. The way a teacher organizes these activities is typically thought of as instructional design. Finally, assessment measures students' status with respect to the curricular aims being sought—for instance, how well students have learned to arrive at accurate mathematical estimates.

Teachers traditionally think of the relationship among curriculum, instruction, and assessment as it is depicted in figure 3.1, where we see that the teacher's initial focus is on curriculum. Attention is then given to the design of instruction. And, finally, near the end of instruction (or sometimes even after it has been completed), attention is given to assessment. Although the sequence in figure 3.1 is traditional, it represents a less than optimal way of thinking about those three activities. The problem arises

FIGURE 3.1   *The Traditional Sequence in Which Teachers Consider Curriculum, Instruction, and Assessment*

because although teachers may sometimes toss token attention to curriculum, as I have been arguing, what most teachers become engrossed in is instruction.

Curriculum gets looked at once over lightly, and assessment is almost forgotten until instruction is nearing the finish line. Although a process of curriculum then instruction then assessment makes logical sense, it is often distorted by well-intentioned teachers who seem to be seduced by the allure of instructional process. Curriculum serves as a typical starting point in a teacher's thinking, but a cavalier consideration of what's to be sought often leads to partially understood curricular intentions, which in turn can result in less than carefully conceived instructional activities. And, of course, assessment is almost always an afterthought because its contributions to instructional planning late in the game are often trivial.

So, in order to dramatically bump up the attention they give to curricular aims, teachers should consider adopting the kind of planning sequence seen in figure 3.2. In this more current conception of how to design instruction, we see that teachers can initially focus on the nature of curricular aims. However, before designing the instruction that's to promote attainment of those aims, teachers actually construct (or at least completely conceptualize) how students' achievement of those curricular aims will be measured. By carefully thinking through the nature of assessment before the instruction is designed, the teacher operationalizes a curricular aim—that is, chooses the operation (such as students' performance on a particular test) that will supply the evidence from which the teacher can infer whether students have attained the desired aim.

Operationalizing a curricular aim by spelling out how students' mastery will be measured is a marvelous way of clarifying what's actually

FIGURE 3.2 *A Contemporary Sequence in Which Teachers Consider Curriculum, Instruction, and Assessment*

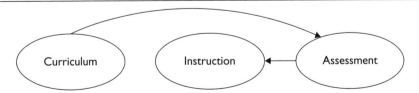

being sought. There's often far too much fuzz on the curricular peaches at which teachers are supposed to aim their instruction. Operationalizing curricular aims via assessment can dramatically reduce that fuzz. And, happily, the resultant heightened clarity can often override a teacher's tendency to get too caught up in instructional process.

When a teacher knows how students' accomplishment of a curricular aim is going to be assessed, and realizes that assessment tools already exist to measure the curricular aim's attainment (or have been thought through completely), it is next to impossible for the teacher to completely overlook the intended ends of instruction. It is this clarity of instructional intent (in the form of operationalized curricular aims) that will typically dissuade a teacher from getting too transfixed by instructional process. Clarified instructional intentions will—and should—govern much of a teacher's instructional thinking.

Evaluating instruction

There's a second reason teachers need to attend to curricular aims, and it flows directly from the underlying function of education. We teach students in order to change them. If a child shows up at school unable to read, then it's the teacher's task to change that child from a nonreader to a reader. If the child ends up as a reader, the teacher's instruction has been successful. If, however, the child remains a nonreader—that is, if the child hasn't been changed by the instruction—then the teaching has flopped.

The key to judging instructional quality is what happens to kids as a consequence of how they've been taught.

And this is why teachers who wish to evaluate their own instruction must be preoccupied not with what happens *during* instruction but, rather, with what has happened to students *after* the instruction is over. Teachers, however, need to judge instruction on the basis of its *effects* on students—both the *intended* effects (embodied in a set of curricular aims) as well as *unintended* effects (perhaps effects that were not foreseen at all). For instance, if an algebra teacher does a crackerjack job in getting students to master the curricular aims set out for an algebra course but, in the process, makes most students *detest* algebra, this sort of unanticipated effect of instruction should certainly be taken into consideration when the algebra teacher's instructional success is evaluated.

Defensible evaluative strategies focused on teachers' effectiveness must *always* deal with unanticipated effects on students as well as with the degree to which students have mastered prespecified curricular aims. Teachers should frequently be asking themselves, "Are there any unforeseen effects of my teaching, either positive or negative, that I should take into consideration when evaluating my instruction?"

There's a classic scene in the film *Jerry McGuire*, where an athlete in the midst of a contract negotiation keeps chanting to his agent, "Show me the money! Show me the money!" What we should be chanting in evaluating a teacher's instruction is, "Show me the evidence!" "Show me the evidence!"

The evidence in this case, however, should be some kind of tangible proof representing the degree to which curricular aims were achieved by a teacher's students. Typically, of course, such evidence will consist of documentation regarding students' performances on one or more assessment instruments—ranging from conventional types of tests all the way to a variety of *alternative* evidence-collecting procedures, such as portfolio assessments or the appraisal of off-campus projects carried out by student groups.

If teachers are evaluating their own instruction with an eye on improving it the next time around (for instance, in the next school year), then their chief concern should be whether evidence from the assessment(s) being used will enable them to infer whether students have mastered a curricular aim. When teachers evaluate their own instruction, they usually can be fairly relaxed about how they assemble and analyze evidence. Their purpose, after all, is simply to shape up their own teaching.

If teachers are being evaluated by others as part of a district or state-level accountability program, however, greater care should be taken with the collection and analysis of evidence. For instance, in most cases it would be advisable to collect both post- and preinstruction test evidence from the same students. Contrasts between the two sets of test scores are clearly more convincing than analyses based only on students' postinstruction performances. If the tests being employed consist exclusively of multiple-choice or true-false items, then it is a simple matter to contrast students' preinstruction and postinstruction scores. But when the tests contain a number of constructed-response items, such as essays or short-answer items, then substantially more attention must be given to scoring students' responses.

In externally dictated evaluation of teachers, care should be taken so that all scoring of students' performances on any constructed-response items is *blind scoring* carried out by individuals (hopefully several) *other* than the teacher who taught the students involved. These measures are intended to eliminate the perception that teachers are not being objective in the way they score their own students' responses.

The way blind scoring typically works is first to code students' pretests and posttests so, at the appropriate time, they can be distinguished from each other. After all the papers have been coded, the pre- and postinstruction papers are mixed together so that those doing the scoring will be unable to tell whether a response was given before or after instruction. All papers are then scored by someone other than the teacher involved, such as other teachers, parents, or members of the business community. After all the papers have been scored, the codes are employed to assign the papers to pretest and posttest groups.

The hope is that the bulk of the superior blind-scored responses will be found in the postinstruction pile of papers. If this strategy shows that the nonpartisan evaluators who blind-scored the tests have judged students' postinstruction responses to be clearly better than their preinstruction responses, it is powerful evidence of the teacher's instructional effectiveness.

So, looking back, we see that if teachers are to design their instruction optimally or to evaluate their instruction accurately, they must routinely attend more seriously to educational ends than to educational means— that is, to the consequences of the instructional process rather than to the instructional process itself. As suggested earlier, this kind of attention is much less common in America's schools than it should be.

Attention to curricular aims will definitely help teachers plan better, and kids benefit from being on the receiving end of more carefully planned instruction. Gathering postinstruction evidence indicating whether curricular aims were achieved will help teachers evaluate their own instruction more accurately. Kids benefit when teachers have accurately judged the caliber of their previous instructional efforts. So, there are clearly two major dividends to be derived if teachers constantly heed the outcomes they hope their instruction will produce in students.

In a fall 2008 issue of *Education Week,* an essay by Alfie Kohn appears under a title that nicely captures the concerns of this chapter: "It's Not What We Teach, It's What They Learn."[1] Kohn's way of thinking about teaching represents an antidote to the third unlearned lesson that

---

SIDEBAR 3.3

Teacher Evaluation: A Truly Tough Task

More than twenty years ago, I was asked to write a chapter for a book describing how teachers ought to be evaluated.[1] This wasn't the first time I had tussled with the topic of teacher evaluation, but it was the first time I had been able to coalesce what I had learned about teacher evaluation during the first thirty years of my career. As a graduate student, you see, one of my first research assignments was to synthesize what had been learned in the first half of the twentieth century about how to evaluate teachers. The assignment took me more than half a year to complete, and it left me completely dismayed about the teacher-evaluation strategies that had been used up until 1950 or so.

What I discovered during my review of teacher-evaluation research from 1900 to 1950 was that there were obvious serious shortcomings in any of the methodological approaches used up to that point. For one thing, most researchers had unsuccessfully tried to find "optimal instructional procedures" which, when used by a teacher, would almost certainly guarantee students' successful learning. Given the many differences among teachers and students, those surefire teaching techniques just didn't exist.

Then there were the ratings of teachers' ability by their supervisors or principals. Those approaches, too, had taken a serious stumble over the years because different supervisors believed teachers should be doing different things in class. An instructional procedure that was lauded by one supervisor might be lambasted by another.

Observational procedures had also proved ineffective. Even highly sophisticated observational systems that called for well-trained observers to record teachers' and students' actions every few seconds had flopped.

So, when I set out in the late eighties to write a chapter on the evaluation of teachers, I did so with considerable trepidation. Yet, given the particulariza-

is the focus of this chapter. He points out how seductive it can be for a teacher to concentrate on what is being done instructionally rather than considering what happens to students as a result of was done instructionally. As he suggests to teachers, "It's easier to concern yourself with teaching than with learning, just as it's more convenient to say the fault lies with people other than you when things go wrong."[2] Neither Kohn

tion of what's involved when we judge teachers, I concluded that the only defensible approach to teacher evaluation would need to embody a judgmental strategy. The judgment-based teacher evaluation (J-BTE) I proposed in 1988 rested on two key tenets: "Tenet 1: J-BTE relies on the pooled professional judgment of educators who have been trained and certified to make defensible judgments regarding teachers' instructional competence. Tenet 2: J-BTE requires that multiple sources of evidence be considered in the context of a teacher's instructional situation."[2]

I now live in Oregon, and I was interested to learn that in an upcoming election there would be a statewide proposition on the ballot calling for teachers not to be paid any longer on the basis of their years of experience and their number of degrees, but on their "classroom performance" (without much explication of what that pithy phrase actually meant). So, I dug out my 20-year-old chapter about teacher evaluation and reread it to see what parts of it, if any, still made sense to me. I found I disagreed very little with what I'd written more than two decades earlier.

I still believe it is impossible to accurately judge teachers' effectiveness based on observations of their classroom behaviors. I still think we need to look at a variety of evidence, then judge the cogency of such evidence according to the particular situations in which individual teachers find themselves. And I still think we dare not use professional educators to render evaluative judgments until they have been trained and certified to tackle this task. Evidence about a teacher's instructional procedures would have a place in what I'd want judges to consider, but it would be far less significant that what happens to kids as a consequence of the instructional procedures being used.

I suppose you could say that I'm just too stubborn to have changed all that much during the past twenty years. Or, it may be more accurate to say that what's really stubborn is the task of evaluating teachers.

nor I is suggesting that teachers give no attention to their instructional planning and delivery, but the payoff must unarguably be what happens to kids after they've been taught.

A LESSON-LEARNT SOLUTION

This specific stumbling block to our schools' success—namely, the preoccupation with instructional process—has been around for a long time. It is such a common mistake that during a number of phases in my own career as an educator, preoccupation with process seemed to be almost universal. Few educators I worked with or even encountered casually seemed to give a hoot about instructional ends. In truth, on the ends-means continuum, I often regarded myself as a confirmed outlier. Fortunately, there seem to be a few positive signs today in Education Land. For instance, as suggested in the preceding chapter, interest among educators in formative assessment appears to be growing. The formative assessment process depends mightily on the use of evidence elicited by assessments of what kids have learned. Therefore, the more often teachers adopt formative assessment in their classrooms, the more certain it is those teachers will attend to the consequences of their teaching rather than to the teaching itself. Nonetheless, the mistake of preoccupation with process is still being made by many teachers and educational administrators. It is a mistake that must be confronted seriously if it is to be remedied.

One factor that has contributed to teachers' undue attention to process is the dreaded enemy of meaningful student learning: content coverage. Many teachers believe, in a profoundly fundamental way, that their chief mission in the classroom is to cover the content that students ought to learn. For example, in a high school history course, the teacher may feel driven to make certain that all significant historical events are covered in class. When teachers set out to cover content at any cost, their focus tends to be on the coverage itself rather than the impact of such coverage, and the cost turns out to be students' reduced understanding of the content covered. Students may experience a fleeting interaction with certain historical events, but most will be forgotten within days, hours, or minutes. If most teachers would take time to find out what their students are getting out of those content-coverage carnivals, teachers would surely cease and desist. Rolling through reams of content may allow teachers to feel they've done what they're supposed to, but it doesn't have a meaningful impact on students.

Another reason we find many teachers preoccupied with instructional process rather than student outcomes is that they rarely have been asked to deal with the consequences of their teaching. Although in the last decade or two we have seen an astonishing increase in the use of external tests, for most of the history of U.S. public schools, only scant attention has been given to educational assessment. So, even though many of today's teachers may be moaning over the amount of testing now imposed on them, this attention to testing is a relatively recent phenomenon. And, of course, old habits of thinking are tough to alter.

Teachers have, probably since the medieval era, spent time thinking, "What will I do with my students tomorrow?" A historical preoccupation with instructional process isn't going to disappear with a snap of the fingers, as established mindsets are rooted out only with great effort. Accordingly, the way we must deal with this process preoccupation is to ready ourselves for a long-term, unrelenting reorientation campaign that I would describe as *augmented incrementalism*.

Augmented incrementalism recognizes that widely held concepts are sometimes adopted without any careful consideration by those doing the adopting. People accept a certain way of viewing the world simply because everyone around them seems to be viewing it that way. Therefore, what is needed is a systematically planned series of catalytic activities to spur a shift in educators' thinking about instructional means and ends. Such an initiative could be spearheaded by a collaboration of national education associations, including, for instance, the National Education Association, the American Federation of Teachers, the American Association of School Administrators, and the Association for Supervision and Curriculum Development. At a summit of leaders from these and other pivotal organizations, certainly including the Council of Chief State School Officers, a low-cost, long-term plan could be devised in which each participating organization would annually undertake activities intended to encourage their members to become more attentive to the consequences of instruction, rather than to instruction per se.

I believe this collaborative initiative need not be costly because many national associations already have a number of dissemination vehicles at their disposal (monthly journals or annual conferences) that could easily (at essentially no cost) include messages regarding the merits of thinking about the consequences of education. For example, commentaries about the dangers of content-coverage instruction could be periodically tossed at readers, reminding them that when they find themselves thinking, "I have to cover this or that content," it is a thought to be vigorously expunged. Too many teachers continue to think that once a topic is touched on in class, albeit superficially and only for a few moments, those teachers are off the hook. Content touched on briefly and superficially does not stick in the skulls of students, to remain there, well learned, forever. Content touched on is not destined to make a difference in students' live.

Another significant contribution to augmented incrementalism could be part of the professional development activities provided for practicing educators by states, districts, or schools. A professional development activity could send a clear message that when teachers focus on instructional process without a concomitant focus on instructional consequences, it is likely to injure children educationally. For instance, professional development aimed at helping groups of teachers at the same grade level or in the same subject area develop common rubrics for assessment can spur them to shift their focus from process to outcomes. Peer observations of classroom teaching, combined with data gathered from student work, can similarly encourage teachers to focus on the effectiveness of different teaching techniques.

In addition, teachers might be given designs for professional development activities focused directly on the instructional role of clear curricular aims. Such activities might deal with specific procedures for using curricular aims to plan effective instruction or evaluate whether instruction has been successful.

There also may be merit in using teacher learning committees to tackle, over an extended period, such thorny issues as how best to assess students' attainment of high-priority curricular aims. Any game plan intended to encourage teachers to be more attentive to curricular ends will be congruent with the chief thrust of classroom formative assessment. As explained in the previous chapter, the formative assessment process is predicated on instructional adjustments that are based on assessment-elicited evidence of students' learning. Thus, formative assessment is dominantly concerned with the ongoing consequences of instruction.

In addition to professional development for the teachers currently staffing our schools, a comparable emphasis on eradicating a preoccupation with process should be taking place in the teacher-education programs that prepare our future teachers. Leaders of teacher-education organizations should, therefore, be encouraged to take part in programs that disabuse prospective teachers of the lure of lavishing too much attention on instructional process.

The overall outcome of an augmented-incrementalism campaign is to get the vast majority of educators to attend sufficiently to instructional consequences so that the success of any instructional procedures will always be determined by what happens to students once these students have been instructed. Such a mind-set on the part of educators is, over time, certain to benefit students.

CHAPTER FOUR

The Absence of
Affective Assessment

In 1956, more than a half-century ago, a soon-to-be-influential book dealing with educational objectives was published. *The Taxonomy of Educational Objectives: Handbook I, The Cognitive Domain,* authored by
the University of Chicago's Benjamin Bloom and four colleagues, provided educators with a convenient way of classifying the objectives (that
is, curricular aims) they wanted their students to accomplish.[1] No such
classification system had previously existed.

Bloom once told me, as we rode together on a shuttle bus leaving a
research conference in the early 1980s, that sales of *The Taxonomy* were
remarkably meager during the first few years after its publication. Its
sales saga shifted substantially a few years later, however, when the federal government began to encourage American educators to evaluate
federally funded programs according to whether behavioral objectives
had been achieved (see chapter 1). Indeed, in the sixties and early seventies, after several years of federal pump-priming, *The Taxonomy* was a
best-seller among educators. During this period, what Bloom and his
coauthors had written about educational objectives played a prominent
role in the way many educators thought about the curricular outcomes
they wanted their students to achieve. Although often not recognized,
one of the most important contributions *The Taxonomy* made was the

way it separated educational objectives into three major categories: cognitive, affective, and psychomotor. This three-way separation caused many educators to think about affective educational objectives, often for the first time.

Cognitive objectives are those dealing with students' intellectual achievements. Examples include memorization of the important punctuation conventions used in written composition, solving multistep mathematical word problems, and composing a powerful persuasive essay.

Affective objectives describe students' attitudes, interests, and values. For example, teachers often want their students to become more interested in certain subjects, such as science, or to enjoy certain education-related activities, such as reading. Such curricular aspirations can be characterized as affective objectives.

Finally, psychomotor objectives refer to the small-motor and large-motor physical skills pursued in our schools. A student's mastery of a small-motor skill, such as becoming adept in the use of a computer keyboard, or a large-motor skill, such as learning how to bounce properly on a trampoline, are examples of psychomotor objectives.

The focus of *The Taxonomy*, however, was almost exclusively on cognitive objectives. Bloom and his coauthors spelled out a six-level hierarchical classification system—that is, a taxonomy—of educational objectives. These ranged from the lowest level of cognitive objectives—namely, knowledge (or recall of memorized information)—to the highest level—namely, evaluation (judgments about the merits of methods and materials for particular purposes). For several decades, this six-level system was employed by thousands of educators to categorize the instructional objectives being pursued in schools, districts, and states. Bloom's hierarchy is still used today to classify cognitive objectives but by far fewer educators than in earlier times.

Taxonomy, even though it dealt predominantly with cognitive objectives, also stimulated a number of educators to give serious thought—typically for the first time—to affective educational objectives, which seemed worthy of attention to at least a small number of educators. (Psychomotor objectives were, then and now, a distant third in the arena of educational objectives.) In 1964, fully eight years after the publication of the cognitive *Taxonomy,* a system dealing with affective objectives was published. Authored by David Krathwohl and two coauthors, the 1964 *Taxonomy of Educational Objectives: Handbook II. Affective Domain* attempted to categorize affective educational objectives and thus show how such objectives might serve educators as instructional targets.[2] Using the same approach as its 1956 predecessor, *Affective Taxonomy* laid out a hierarchical classification scheme for affective objectives. This system spelled out five levels ranging from the lowest level—namely, receiving (students are aware of certain stimuli and willing to attend to them)—to the highest level—namely, characterization (a student's values become so pervasive that the student can be characterized by those values).

Although the publication of *Affective Taxonomy* stimulated a degree of additional interest among educators, the new volume did not have the impact of its 1956 cognitive cousin. One suspects that—in the late sixties and early seventies—American educators were beginning to experience pressures, both public and governmental, to increase their students' *cognitive* achievements in the form of higher scores on standardized achievement tests. In contrast, no such pressures surfaced calling for educators to bring about worthwhile *affective* changes in their students. Indeed, if we were to magically create our own taxonomy of difference-making books about educational objectives, we would surely have to place the 1956 *Cognitive Taxonomy* somewhere in the most-influential category, while assigning the 1964 *Affective Taxonomy* to a much lower difference-making level. The modest impact of Krathwohl's *Affective Taxonomy* is regrettable.

AFFECTIVE CURRICULAR AIMS: CAN WE ADVOCATE WHAT WE DON'T ASSESS?

If you were to ask many of today's teachers about the educational importance of affective curricular aims, most of those teachers would indicate that the affective outcomes of education are important. I think they're right. If a child masters mathematics cognitively, but learns to detest mathematics in the process, is the child well served educationally? If kids learn to become genuinely skilled readers, but end up regarding reading as a wretched and repugnant activity, should educators really be elated with this result?

Despite fairly widespread acceptance of the educational significance of affect, we rarely see teachers actively pursuing affective curricular aims in their classrooms. One important reason for this inattention to affect is because we rarely assess students' affective status. Unassessed curricular aims are doomed to be overlooked. This is definitely true in the case of affect.

This, then, is a fourth mistake that's impeding genuine educational success in our schools. Although the absence of affective assessment is rarely recognized as a serious shortcoming in how we educate children, I believe that, in the long term, it is one of the more significant errors that educators continue to make. Here's the mistake, put simply: the affective consequences of education, although astonishingly important, are not pursued by most teachers because students' affective status is never assessed.

It has often been stated, with good reason, that we measure what we treasure. So, because affective outcomes are not measured in our schools, an unmistakable message is sent to those who staff the schools—namely, that the affective consequences of schooling are not important, at least not important enough to measure. Tragically, this is absolutely the wrong message to send to teachers because the affective conse-quences of schooling are enormously significant. If we can educate stu-dents who love to learn, most of them will go on learning. And love of learning is, of course, an affective consequence of schooling that must be zealously sought.

Recently we have seen increasing interest in the notion of student engagement. This may or may not be considered an affective variable, depending on how one defines engagement. If, for example, *engagement* is defined as a student's participation in a wide range of activities at school, both curricular and extracurricular, and establishing a sufficient number of relationships with other students, then it would probably not be regarded as affective but as a participatory variable of some sort. On the other hand, if engagement is regarded as the degree to which a stu-dent really feels hooked into what's going on academically and feels like a bona fide part of classroom activities, then it would fall into the affective realm. This illustrates the need to be particularly clear-headed and rigorous as we try to describe what's meant by students' affect.

The nature of students' affect

Before pitching a proposed solution to correct this fourth unlearned lesson, it will be useful if I clarify just what's meant by affect. Here goes.

Affective variables are those non-cognitive dispositions that influence the behavior of human beings—in many instances, that *strongly* influence such behavior. The kinds of affective variables typically of concern to teachers are students' attitudes, interests, and values. A key word in the sentence-before-last, at least in my view, was *dispositions*. Affective variables dispose individuals to behave in certain ways. Consider figure 4.1 for a moment and you'll see that a person's current affective status is predictive, often powerfully, of that person's future behavior. The attitudes, interests, and values a student currently possesses, therefore, typically serve as meaningful predictors of that student's future conduct.

Consider, for example, a young girl (we'll call her Janie) who currently is quite interested in reading—especially in reading stories about the nineteenth-century women who helped settle the American West. Contrast Janie with her classmate Clare, who, although equally skilled at reading, really doesn't like to read. So, Clare is currently uninterested in reading and Janie is currently interested. Okay, flashing forward ten years, predict which of the two girls will end up reading more. Clearly we should bet on Janie, as children's affective status predisposes them to behave in certain ways when they're older, which is why affective variables are so important. Therefore we should focus on getting children interested in reading because we think it will benefit them in the future.

FIGURE 4.1   *The Predictive Relationship between Students' Current Affective Status and Their Future Behavior*

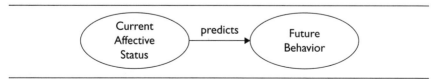

Schools are the mechanisms by which a society prepares its young for the future—for a future well beyond the moment their formal schooling comes to a close. Surely we want students to acquire the cognitive skills and knowledge they'll need during that long-term future, but just as surely we want them to leave school with the affective dispositions that will incline them to use their acquired cognitive skills and knowledge for the rest of their lives.

Another affective variable educators should be concerned with is academic efficacy; that is, the degree to which students believe they are capable of accomplishing the academic tasks they routinely encounter in school. It should be clear that students who believe they are academically capable will typically tend to tackle academic work with more enthusiasm than students who have a low sense of their academic efficacy. The stronger a student's sense of academic efficacy, other things being equal, the more willing that student will be to tackle new academic challenges. In the long run, academically confident students are apt to take on more academic challenges and more likely to be academically successful. Yes, students' affect can have a substantial impact on many aspects of their education.

As one last example, many educators believe they will be more successful if their students are meaningfully engaged in the learning process—actively involved in trying to master a skill or acquire a body of knowledge—rather than merely being passive recipients of teacher-dispensed truths. Accordingly, as indicated earlier, some teachers are now giving particular attention to student *engagement*. Clearly, student *engagement* is an affective rather than cognitive variable—and an important affective variable at that.

When teachers are asked to identify the affective outcomes they'd like their students to attain, they typically describe student *attitudes*, such as a (1) positive attitude toward learning, (2) more positive attitudes toward themselves (i.e., heightened self-esteem), and (3) more appropriate attitudes toward others whose backgrounds are different than their own. Another category of affective variables teachers identify is student *interests*, such as an interest in physics or algebra. A third category is student *values*, such as honesty, integrity, and justice. Clearly, a wide range of affective targets can be adopted as important curricular aims.

But when are teachers ever urged to get serious about promoting their students' affect? In my experience, an administrator might make a few verbal nods in support of affective outcomes during an orientation meeting for a new school year. For example, I've heard some school superintendents urge educators to be attentive to students' attitudes toward learning or to their sense of safety while in school. Yet, when school actually gets under way, talk about affect is soon shunted to the bottom of the curriculum cupboard. When instruction really gets rolling, the pursuit of cognitive curricular aims not only predominates, it almost always drives out any attention to affective outcomes.

So, despite occasional pep talks about the significance of affective outcomes, I've rarely seen systematic, sustained attention given to affective curricular aims. The reason for this is always the same: we talk about affect, but we don't measure students' affective status.

Assessing students' affect

Measuring students' status relative to affective curricular aims is decidedly different than measuring their status regarding cognitive aims. Let's look briefly at the most significant differences between those two assessment strategies.

When we want to determine a student's mastery of a cognitive skill, such as being able to multiply pairs of double-digit numbers, we present a series of appropriate multiplication problems to see how well this particular student can carry out this specific task. Based on the student's success in coping with a sample of, say, ten such problems, we arrive at an inference about his or her mastery of this skill. Because students are supposed to do as well as they can, we hope to determine each student's optimal level of performance. What we are trying to arrive at is an inference about *each individual student's* ability to multiply pairs of double-digit numbers.

As indicated in chapter 2, all assessments of students' mastery of a cognitive curricular aim are based using on their *overt* test performance to make inferences about their *covert* skills or knowledge. Indeed, the thrust of all educational testing involves making score-based inferences about particular students. When a teacher asks students to write several narrative essays, he or she is attempting to make an inference about each student's ability to write narrative essays. Teachers employ cognitive tests exclusively to arrive at valid score-based inferences about individual students.

But, in marked contrast, affective assessment is aimed at making a valid inference about a *group* of students. Teachers who measure students' affect can make inferences about the affective status of a group, but they can't do so for a particular student. Here's why.

Unlike cognitive assessment, where we ask students to *do their best* on a test and thus display their optimal level of performance, in affective assessment we ask students to *tell the truth* as they respond to anonymous self-report inventories (or, if you prefer, self-report questionnaires). Affective inventories must be completed anonymously to minimize a student's likelihood of giving a response intended to please others—for instance, the teacher. If students' anonymous responses are to be useful, they must be honest. Looking at the kinds of items shown below in this self-report inventory about classroom climate, you can see why it would be important for student responses to be anonymous.

The Climate in Our Classroom

Directions: Please circle a response at the right of each statement to show whether you agree with the statement. Please do not give your name, or make any comments on this inventory.

Statements	Circle One		
1. More than half of the time, I am really interested in what's going on in this class.	Agree	Disagree	Uncertain
2. I think my teacher treats me and all the other students in our class very fairly.	Agree	Disagree	Uncertain

10. Our teacher thinks if certain kids are smart, they don't need to work hard.	Agree	Disagree	Uncertain

Because the most direct way to get an accurate fix on students' affective status is to ask them to respond to items in a self-report inventory, and because those responses must be made anonymously in order to minimize socially desirable responses, we cannot make any inferences about an individual student's affect because, obviously, we don't know which student responded to which of the self-report inventories. If we were to tell students to put their names on affective inventories, it is far too likely that those students (knowing their responses would be identified) would respond in ways they believe a teacher would want them to respond. We might know which students made which responses, but we wouldn't have any confidence in what those responses actually meant.

However, there are still substantial instructional dividends if teachers can get a reasonably accurate fix on the affective status of their entire class, and this is precisely how they can use self-report inventories— to make inferences about their students' attitudes, interests, and values, as a group. Based on students' average responses to a self-report inventory (always an anonymous one), a teacher can discern the affective status of the entire group, thereby helping the teacher to deal instructionally with factors relevant to promoting particular affective curricular aims.

I'm certain it's clear that the evidence acquired by using affective inventories is not intended to evaluate, grade, or even instruct individual students. Rather, this evidence is intended for the teacher's use in designing an appropriate educative experience for the entire group of students for whom the teacher is responsible.

For instance, suppose a teacher discovers that most students hold a low estimation of their own academic efficacy—that is, they believe they are essentially unable to accomplish the kinds of tasks they are asked to carry out in school. With information gathered from the inventory, the teacher could attempt to boost students' academic confidence, and thus their efficacy—for instance, by stressing their past academic accomplishments or structuring tasks to ensure that students are more likely to experience success. Serious shortcomings in students' sense of academic efficacy demand serious efforts on the part of the teacher. Such efforts will increase the likelihood that students are successful in carrying out their routine academic assignments.

But, you might be wondering, even with anonymous inventories, won't some students still give less than honest responses? Won't some students fear that any negative responses from a group, even if made with complete anonymity, might negatively dispose a teacher toward the entire class? Yes, those of us who have taught for any length of time have certainly encountered students who believe it best to offend no one, especially the teacher.

It is almost impossible to completely expunge vestiges of social desirability from students' responses—even if those responses are anonymous. Some answers will likely be more positive than they would have been if the student had been totally honest. Others are likely to be tilted in a negative direction. (Surely some students may use the cloak of anonymity to engage in some sort of retribution toward the teacher.) Taken together, however, at least some too-positive responses will be cancelled out by some too-negative ones. What a teacher ends up with may not be perfect, but it will provide a serviceably accurate estimate of the average affective status among this group of students. Inferences based on this information can help teachers decide if they need to attend instructionally to any curricular aims dealing with affect.

In figure 4.2, you will find an example of an inventory teachers can use to get a fix on their students' affect—in this instance, students in upper elementary school (grades 4–6)—toward certain aspects of school. The inventory was designed to have students respond to a pair of statements (one framed positively and one negatively) on three subjects (mathematics, social studies, and science), and to a pair of statements about three salient skills students need to acquire (writing, reading, and giving oral presentations). There are also two statements (the first and last in the inventory) aimed at gauging students' reactions to school in general.

As you can see from glancing at figure 4.2, this sort of inventory can be constructed without Herculean effort, yet can yield useful information for teachers. Suppose, for instance, a teacher reviews thirty students' responses to the inventory in figure 4.2 and discovers that most of them disagree with Statement 2, "I enjoy learning about scientific things," but agree with Statement 8, "I don't ever want to become a scientist." This sort of response pattern should suggest to the teacher that whatever is going on during science instruction seems to be fostering in students a

p 86

FIGURE 4.2 *An Illustrative Affective Self-Report Inventory*

My View of School

Directions: Please indicate whether you agree with the statements in this inventory. Some of the statements are positive and some are negative. Decide whether you agree with each statement. There are no right or wrong answers, so answer honestly. Please do not write your name on the inventory. Only make X marks.
Here is a sample:

	Response (one per statement)		
Statements	**I agree.**	**I disagree.**	**I'm unsure.**
I like to watch TV.	☒	☐	☐

After you finish, a student will collect all the inventories and place them in a sealed envelope that will be taken by that same student directly to the principal's office. Thanks for your help!

	Response (one per statement)		
Statements	**I agree.**	**I disagree.**	**I'm unsure.**
1. Most of the time, I like school a lot.	☐	☐	☐
2. I enjoy learning about scientific things.	☐	☐	☐
3. If asked to, I can write good reports.	☐	☐	☐
4. Actually, I don't much like to read.	☐	☐	☐
5. I don't like to speak in front of my class.	☐	☐	☐
6. I think doing mathematics is fun.	☐	☐	☐
7. I enjoy learning about social studies.	☐	☐	☐
8. I don't ever want to become a scientist.	☐	☐	☐
9. I truly don't enjoy writing things.	☐	☐	☐
10. If I have the time, I like to read books.	☐	☐	☐
11. I enjoy speaking in front of an audience.	☐	☐	☐
12. I definitely don't like doing math.	☐	☐	☐
13. When we do social studies, I don't like it.	☐	☐	☐
14. Generally, I don't enjoy school very much.	☐	☐	☐

negative affect toward science. Clearly, this provides a clue that some adjustments are needed to help students' develop more positive attitudes toward science.

An inventory can include more items per affective variable—for instance, two or three times as many statements as the pair of statements seen in figure 4.2. But even with only a pair of items per affective variable, the teacher can get a rough notion of students' affect and can act on this information.

To sum up, it is possible for teachers to snare meaningful insights about their students by reaching inferences based on the entire groups' responses to anonymous self-report affective inventories. Figure 4.2 provides an example of what self-report inventories might look like. Although paying greater attention to the construction of affective inventories will obviously improve their quality, the cost of affective self-report inventories is relatively modest. The topic of assessing students' affect is treated at greater length in several sources.[3]

The instructional impact of upcoming affective assessment

One remarkable dividend of affective assessment is that the prospect of its occurrence can alter the way teachers teach. Imagine that you are a high school English teacher and your principal has directed you to collect both pre- and postinstruction affective evidence from your students. The principal has given you the affective inventory, which is focused on how confident your students are regarding two key communication skills, namely, the ability to make oral presentations to other students and the ability to write brief explanatory essays. What the principal appears to be looking for, based on the use of this inventory, is a marked increase in your students' confidence in their speaking and writing skills.

By now it's clear that because of this impending comparison of your students' pre-and postinstruction confidence in their skills, you will almost certainly pay more attention to the two affective variables during your day-to-day instruction than you otherwise might have done. This is why: impending assessment galvanizes a teacher's attention to the affective variables slated to be assessed.

But even if there were no external imposition of affective assessment on teachers, such as by a school's principal in the foregoing hypothetical example, the galvanizing impact of impending affective assessment can still be profound even if a teacher assesses affect without being coerced to do so. Suppose, for instance, that you are a fifth-grade teacher who has decided to measure your students' perceived sense of academic engagement at the end of a school year. You're not directed to do this

P 89

SIDEBAR 4.1

Sending Societal Expectations

I have always thought that when we attempt to measure students' affect, we send educators an important message, namely, that our society expects its schools not only to teach the 3Rs but also to promote appropriate student affect. Societal expectations are potent and they can alter people's behaviors. I can recount a personal experience to illustrate this point.

Most of my life, because I've been faced with many commitments, I've tried to use my time shrewdly. To illustrate, during my nearly thirty years on the UCLA faculty, I tried to snare spare minutes whenever I could. I relied on one of my favorite time-saving ploys as I drove the streets of Los Angeles. Whenever I was waiting at a traffic signal at the head of the left-turn line, I found that when the signal changed from red to green and the autos heading in the opposite direction (that is, toward me) did not move instantly, I could turn left before they got under way, thus avoiding any delay. I probably saved about three seconds every time I was able to make one of these rapid-response left-hand turns, so I foresaw that, over the course of a lifetime, I could save at least fifteen minutes or so. I felt that forced waiting was foolish if one could avoid it.

Okay, so one evening I was returning to my home in the San Fernando Valley, having just picked up a bucket of chicken from KFC. (This was so long ago that KFC was still known as Kentucky Fried Chicken.) Anyway, I was on Ventura Boulevard, waiting at the head of the left-turn line. When the traffic light changed from red to green, my upcoming "opponents" dawdled, hence I made my customary lightning left turn. Having been so successful over the years in accomplishing this suave maneuver, I thought nothing of it.

But then, after about three blocks, I was pulled over by a police car whose blaring siren and flashing lights signaled to me that something was definitely

continued

SIDEBAR 4.1   *continued*

wrong. I did not know what it was. I rolled down the window and waited as an LAPD officer approached my car. He seemed to be straight out of central casting, a large man wearing polished boots, a nicely pressed uniform, sun glasses, and a holstered handgun. He also had a meaningfully bushy moustache. I assure you that I regarded him with seriousness, even though I still did not sense why he pulled me over.

I will never forget his opening words —"Okay, Bucko, you pulled a jack-rabbit back there"—because I had absolutely no idea what he meant. Was the policeman telling me that I had inadvertently run over a creature of the forest? Was I to be accused of practicing magic without a license? I truly did not know what his words meant. So I asked.

"Pulled a jack rabbit?" I said, querulously. His reply was instantaneous: "You pulled a jack-rabbit left turn back there, Buck!" I noticed that he had shifted his form of address from "Bucko" to "Buck," and I was instantly impressed with his flexibility. He went on to explain that jack-rabbit left turns were illegal in California. I believed him, and meekly accepted my ticket. I tend to be particularly malleable when confronted with loaded weapons.

Well, I was notified by mail of the fine for my left-turn sin. As I recall, it was about $40. That seemed reasonable to me, and I sent in the check promptly. What seemed far less reasonable took place two months later, when my auto insurance bill arrived. It appears that my Ventura Blvd. driving mistake had been the third offence in a two-year span, which put me into a decidedly more costly insurance-premium category. My annual auto insurance premium had tripled—a bump of more than $800!

Society had sent me an unequivocal message. Jack-rabbit left turns were illegal, and I immediately stopped making them. Actually, for almost a full year, I never turned left at all! If you make three right-hand turns, you can go anywhere you want in America.

When significant educational tests are looming, such as the accountability tests currently used throughout the nation, those tests send a strong message to teachers that whatever is being measured should be learned by students. If the accountability tests are appropriate and their content defensible, this is a potent way to let educators know what society regards as significant. Educators can, and should, attend to what's being assessed. Similarly, if society told educators that students' affect was important enough to warrant its assessment, then educators would surely promote students' acquisition of the affective qualities to be assessed.

kind of measurement, you just think it is an important thing to do. You have created a ten-item self-report inventory focused on various aspects of students' academic engagement. By using this inventory, you hope to come up with a valid group-focused inference about whether your students believe they are meaningfully engaged with the instruction and learning that's taking place in your class. No one is forcing you; you've done this simply because you believe that increasing students' academic engagement is a worthwhile curricular aim, and you want to assess your students' level of engagement by measuring their status at the close of the term. You might also decide to use your inventory as a pretest at the beginning of the term, and then contrast students' pre- and postinstruction responses. How you use your newly developed affective inventory is up to you, and you alone.

Even if the idea of measuring your students' affect is entirely your own, you are certain to be influenced by the nature of what's going to be assessed. You will almost certainly try to do things in class that will nurture your students' academic engagement. When we treasure something enough to measure it, then we put extra instructional attention into it.

So, affective assessment not only allows teachers to detect whether affective curricular aims are being achieved, it also sends a strong signal to teachers that what's being assessed is worth their instructional attention.

Looking at the logic trail

Let me briefly recapitulate the underlying logic associated with this fourth unlearned lesson, an error of omission wherein educators simply do not assess their students' affective status.

- First, students' affect is unarguably important and, therefore, can play a prominent role not only in how students are learning but also in influencing significant aspects of their future behavior.

- Second, because essentially no assessment of students' affect takes place in our schools, we see scant instructional attention given by teachers to the promotion of affective curricular aims.

- Third, students' affective status can be economically assessed using anonymous self-report inventories, and the resulting group-focused inferences can help teachers adjust their instruction so students accomplish their affective curricular aims.

- Finally, facing upcoming affective assessments will stimulate teachers to devote increased instructional attention to the type of affective outcomes to be assessed.

If you don't find any serious gaps in this trail of logic, it should be clear by now why our continuing reluctance to assess students' affect represents a fourth—and formidable—mistake. It's a mistake we should rectify.

A LESSON-LEARNT SOLUTION

Happily, the solution to this fourth unlearned lesson is straightforward. To implement it is, arguably, the easiest of this book's six lesson-learnt solutions. It is a simple two-step solution, but both steps must be carried out in order to fix this error of omission. Let's look now at these two steps.

Step I: Provision of optional affective assessment inventories

I indicated earlier that the creation of affective self-report inventories is a relatively low-cost undertaking. And it is. Any reader of this book could, if motivated, sit down and churn out an affective assessment inventory in relatively short order. I think the resulting inventory would be useful and, if actually employed with students, in most instances would lead to improved instruction. But, clearly, an affective inventory spun out by novice inventory-builders is apt to contain the sort of assessment mistakes one would expect.

For example, the phrasing of the inventory items (typically, the sorts of agree-disagree statements you saw in figure 4.2) is mighty important. To illustrate, suppose an affective inventory is being used with high school students who must signify their agreement with a series of statements, such as "I think school, much of the time, is really interesting." In response to the statement, students are to select one of the following options: Strongly Agree, Agree, Uncertain, Disagree, or Strongly Disagree. But suppose the person generating the inventory phrased this statement in a way that was so positive or so negative that almost all students were likely to respond the same way. For example, suppose the above statement read, "I think school, all of the time, is the very most interesting place I can ever be." Certainly few students—at least the ones

I know—would ever agree with this excessively goody-goody assertion. Or, let's say the statement was much too negative: "I think school, every minute I am in it, is the most detestable place I could ever be." Few students think that every minute of their school day is so vile that they'd agree with this statement. In most schools, after all, there is recess! For the purpose of analysis, if the items in an affective inventory fail to yield sufficient differences among students' responses, then the inventory will be of little use because we can't distinguish satisfactorily among students' differing affective dispositions.

It should be clear, then, that if an affective inventory is going to be first rate, substantial care must be given to the way each item is phrased. Moreover, even carefully crafted inventories are rarely perfect the first time they are created. Ideally, therefore, affective inventories must be tried out, revised, tried out, revised, and so on, until they are as polished as possible. But giving serious attention to developing affective inventories is not something an already busy teacher has the time or the experience—much less the inclination—to do. If we sit back and wait for our already harassed teaching force to generate its own affective assessments, we'll be waiting forever.

Accordingly, the first step in my recommended two-step solution to this unlearned lesson is that optional affective assessment inventories should be developed, refined, and placed at the disposal of teachers. Whether or not teachers want to use those inventories should be up to them. Ideally, the inventories would be constructed so that teachers could modify them to mesh better with a teacher's preferences regarding the measurement of particular affective outcomes. But the choice of whether to employ any of these optional affective inventories, with or without adaptations, should be the teacher's.

Who, then, would be constructing these affective inventories? Well, this is a task ideally suited to federal or state education agencies—or possibly to research-and-development centers funded by state or federal governments. The challenge, of course, is to create assessments that address the most common kinds of affective variables that teachers are apt to pursue.

Great care must be taken not to develop inventories for assessing any affective variables that engender controversy. The measurement of students' affect is not an opportunity to promote some sort of surreptitious, value-laden political agenda. Measurement of affective variables that, in the eyes of citizens, are best left to the family or to religious organizations should never be undertaken. Yet, identifying the affective variables that are of most interest to educators in a given school or district should not be particularly difficult. Refinement of affective inventories can take time and, depending on the magnitude of the refinement, could easily become expensive. However, if spaced out over several years, such try-out-revision cycles of affective inventories need not be very costly.

Another possibility for the production of such affective inventories is for one or more private foundations to underwrite the generation of these sorts of assessments. In recent years, many major philanthropic organizations have turned their attention to the improvement of public schooling. By supplying designated dollars to educational agencies for inventory construction, a private foundation could take a significant leadership position in the generation of difference-making affective inventories for the nation's schools.

As soon as a sufficient array of optional affective inventories is available, the educators who might want to use them should be notified of the availability of such assessment tools. These inventories would be, in essence, governmentally or privately produced assessment tools put in the hands of teachers and school administrators with the hope, but not the demand, that the tools would be used. Let's turn, then, to the second step in my solution strategy to address this longstanding error of omission.

Step 2: Affect-focused professional development

The vast majority of educators know almost nothing about either the assessment of students' affect or how to promote students' attainment of affective curricular aims. Teachers in training get no serious instruction dealing with student affect, nor do teachers, once they tumble into the trenches. Thus, the second step in getting more teachers to attend to students' affective status is to provide at least a modest amount of professional development—to show teachers first how to measure student affect and then how to interpret students' responses. In addition, affect-related professional development programs should deal with how teachers can modify students' affective dispositions.

Understandably, teachers aren't going to be willing to measure their students' affect if they don't understand anything about affect or how to assess it. Similarly, how many teachers are likely to deal with affective assessments if they have no idea how to alter students' affect? After all, the instructional tactics that are suitable for promoting students' mastery of cognitive objectives are really quite different from the instructional tactics to be used when trying to modify students' affective dispositions. Teachers need to acquire a repertoire of instructional techniques, such as modeling the desired affect, which can lead to appropriate affective shifts among their students.

Acquiring a repertoire of instructional tactics to influence affect is a task ideally suited for teacher learning community (teachers only) and professional learning communities (teachers and administrators). Over a single school year, a school's educators can become well versed in the assessment of students' affect and how, once assessment tools are in place, to bring about worthwhile changes in students' attitudes, interests, and values.

Without both of these steps—that is, the distribution of optional assessment tools and the provision of professional development activities necessary to use the results of those assessments effectively—I fear this will continue to be an unlearned lesson. This mistake—inattention to affect—can cost children the kind of rich, useful education they should be getting. Educators should treasure students' affect enough to measure it. And, once measured, educators should attend instructionally to promoting appropriate affect.

CHAPTER FIVE

Instructionally Insensitive Accountability Tests

If you had a friend who, suspecting he had a fever, tried to take his temperature by hopping onto his bathroom scales, you'd probably conclude he was in serious need of some smarten-up pills. People who measure things with the wrong measurement devices display decisively diminished capacities.

Well, from the earliest beginnings of the educational accountability movement in America—a movement nearly a half-century old by now—we've been judging the quality of America's schools using the wrong measurement tools. We've been evaluating our schools using students' scores on tests that are flat-out faulty for that function. We've been using tests that are incapable of distinguishing between successfully and unsuccessfully taught students. In many instances, we could have done almost as well by using a set of bathroom scales.

AN EXERCISE IN ABSURDITY

Let's spend a moment considering a situation that would be almost laughable, were it not educationally harmful to so many students. As might be expected, that situation arises from the fifth of the unlearned lessons I'm tangling with in this book. The specific mistake I highlight in this chapter is this: most of America's educational accountability programs rely on tests that are incapable of determining how well students have been taught.

The reason educational accountability programs exist, of course, is that someone doubts—that is, someone in a position of authority doubts—whether a particular educational program is doing a good job. Incredulity about quality, in fact, is the rationale underlying all account- ability programs—in education or elsewhere. Here's why. If sufficient numbers of stakeholders become doubtful about the performances of any service providers, for instance, the services provided by police officers or trash collectors, those stakeholders typically will, at some point, install procedures requiring evidence of the quality of the service rendered. If enough taxpayers begin to doubt that educators are getting good results from the tax dollars being spent on schools, it is almost certain that some form of educational accountability will be imposed on those educators.

I suspect that if we could go back in history, we'd find that there has always been some level of carping about the instructional quality pro- vided by certain teachers. Yet, the occasional poor teacher notwithstand- ing, for many years most Americans regarded U.S. public schools as one of the nation's crowing achievements. When I was going through the public schools in Portland, Oregon, my parents and I never heard com- plaints that they were inadequate. Oh, sure, there might have been a clunker school or two, and certainly a few teachers were better suited for other jobs. But, by and large, Americans were both pleased with and proud of their nation's public schools.

State educational accountability programs

In the 1950s, however, murmurs of discontent with our schools could definitely be discerned. In 1955, for instance, Rudolph Flesch wrote a widely read book, *Why Johnny Can't Read,* in which he argued that because many students were being taught to use a "look-say" approach to reading, they were not learning how to read.[1] As the 1960s arrived, we began to hear more and more complaints from the business commu- nity about high school graduates who couldn't properly fill out job- application forms or write coherent sentences. In newspapers, letters to the editors bemoaned the social promotion of students based on "seat time" rather than academic achievement. Minor doubts about the qual- ity of America's public schools were becoming major doubts.

Soon, public distress with the quality of our tax-supported schools reached a level where state legislatures began to enact laws establishing accountability programs whose sole function was to give policymakers (for instance, members of the board of education or the legislature) hard evidence regarding students' achievement levels. By the time the 1970s rolled around, it was generally accepted that the way to evaluate schools was to make students take achievement tests, then to use the scores on those tests as indicators of a school's instructional effectiveness. If students scored well on such tests, it was thought that this evidence indicated successful instruction. But if students scored poorly on the tests, the opposite conclusion was reached.

This expansion of state-level accountability programs continued apace through the late seventies and early eighties. In some states, students' scores on these accountability tests were linked to the awarding of high school diplomas or grade promotion. But educators in essentially all fifty states found that an accountability program had been laid on them by state authorities—sometimes gently, sometimes harshly. And, without exception, those programs were structured around test-based accountability.

Federal statutes fostering test-based evaluation

It is apparent, then, that growing concerns about U.S. public schools triggered a state-by-state legislative response in the form of test-based accountability programs. A number of those approaches were stringent; a number were soft. But state lawmakers realized voters wanted evidence that their schools were working properly. This spate of state-spawned programs to evaluate public schools was, clearly, a powerful element of America's educational accountability movement. But there was another factor spurring the emergence of educational accountability, namely, federal law. And one federal law in particular, a statute enacted by Congress in 1965 and reauthorized eight times since, has played a prominent role in shaping what Americans think about their schools and how to evaluate them.

In 1965, the Elementary and Secondary Education Act (ESEA), a key component of President Lyndon Johnson's Great Society, was enacted. This landmark law gave states unprecedented levels of federal dollars—chiefly with the intention of obliging state educators to do a better job of teaching economically disadvantaged students who historically had not been well served by the public schools. Because the money for public schools had been supplied almost exclusively by state and local governments prior to

ESEA's enactment, this new law (and its substantial dollars) made a real difference in the way U.S. educators began to pay for their instructional programs and how they began to think about them. Robert Kennedy, in 1965 the junior U.S. senator from New York, argued effectively in Congress that the considerable tax dollars being doled out to the states by ESEA should be carefully evaluated so that each state's federal funding in the coming year would be dependent on evidence that this year's ESEA-supported programs had been effective. As a consequence, ESEA soon stimulated hitherto unseen interest in the use of test-based evidence to evaluate the effectiveness of education.

The 1994 reauthorization of ESEA, known as the Improving America's Schools Act (IASA), emphasized even more than earlier ESEA reauthorizations the significance of students' test performances in determining whether the nation's students had achieved the skills and knowledge they were supposed to achieve. Under IASA, state recipients of federal funding were obliged to collect evidence that students had achieved their state's "challenging" curricular goals. This altered view of how states should employ their accountability test data meshed well with most state accountability programs. IASA's endorsement of test-based evaluations of school effectiveness was seen by many state education policymakers as an official (federal) vindication of their reliance on test-based evidence to determine whether their schools were working properly.

In the most recent reauthorization of ESEA, the 2002 No Child Left Behind Act (NCLB), the role of test-based school evaluations became dramatically more reified than in any previous incarnations of ESEA. NCLB not only more than doubled the number of required tests, it also established stringent regulations regarding how those tests were to be built and, thereafter, how the tests' results were to be used. Even NCLB's most vocal critics, however, typically approved of its overall goal of trying to ensure that all students were well educated. Other features of NCLB also received applause, such as its required disaggregation of certain student subgroups' test performance. On the other hand, opponents of NCLB contended that the law's target of getting all U.S. students to attain realistic levels of test-determined proficiency by 2014 was altogether unrealistic.

The accountability strategy in NCLB, even more than in IASA, was based on three assumptions: (1) students' achievement levels should improve; (2) students' scores on state-determined, federally approved accountability tests can identify the districts and schools whose students have not been effectively educated; and (3) corrective action can be taken to improve the instructional effectiveness of low-scoring districts and schools. Because schools and districts whose students failed to make "adequate yearly progress" (AYP) on their state's NCLB tests were subjected to a series of federally prescribed penalties, the overriding accountability mantra for many educators morphed into a unitary focus: "Raise test scores to dodge AYP failure!"

The nation's report card

The National Assessment of Educational Progress (NAEP) is another federal initiative that has influenced the way we think about how to evaluate our schools most effectively. Referred to as the Nation's Report Card by those who operate it, NAEP has been around since 1969. In its early years, NAEP's role was to trace the assessed performance of U.S. students over the years. Any recommendations that NAEP should function in an evaluative capacity were roundly rejected. Indeed, because in the early years NAEP results were reported only at a regional level—for instance, in the southeastern region—no evaluation of any states or districts was possible. In its early years, NAEP was definitely a low-stakes or, possibly, a no-stakes test.

NAEP employs a carefully designed sampling strategy to identify potential examinees, as well as a test-administration procedure calling for different test-takers to complete only a subsection of each year's test. This "matrix" sampling strategy allows the gathering of representative student test performance data based on decisively less administrative time than would otherwise be the case. However, the use of matrix sampling makes it impossible to accurately compare individual students' test performances with one another. Since 1990, however, it has been possible for NAEP to collect data and report results on a state-by-state basis so that students' scores in one state can be contrasted with those in other states. (Starting in 2002, NAEP scores were also reported for a number of urban school districts.)

NCLB included a provision making it obligatory for states to take part in state-by-state NAEP comparisons. Because NAEP is generally perceived to be a nonpartisan and technically sound test, policymakers in many states have begun to view NAEP results as the "real" evidence of the effectiveness of their public schools. Even though district-level or school-level results are not reported (except in a handful of urban school districts), the comparison of a state's NAEP results with the results of its own accountability tests has led to disputes regarding, for instance, the number of students who are classified as proficient on the two assessments. With few exceptions, more students are designated proficient (and above) by state tests than by NAEP tests. Such inconsistencies tend to erode the credibility of one—or both—of these types of tests.

An underlying assumption: is it warranted?

It is a fundamental premise of NCLB that high scores on a state's accountability test are indicative of satisfactory instruction. In other words, it is believed that high-scoring students have been well taught, whereas low-scoring students have not been well taught. It is assumed, therefore, that students' scores on NCLB accountability tests are accurately reflective of instructional quality. But what if this assumption were flagrantly false?

What if the teachers and administration in a school serving disadvantaged students actually teach their students spectacularly well but those students' scores do not improve on annual NCLB tests? Or what if students in an affluent suburban school district invariably earn top scores on yearly accountability tests, even though the instruction provided by their teachers is decidedly mediocre? Those are two significant what ifs!

But the answer to both of those "what ifs" is the same. If effectively taught students' accountability test scores don't improve or if ineffectively taught students' still score well, two things will certainly happen. First, schools will be inaccurately evaluated so that the wrong schools get chastised and the wrong schools are praised. Second, many students will be educationally harmed because their teachers will choose inappropriate ways to prepare students for dysfunctional accountability tests.

First off, if students' test scores do not accurately indicate teachers' instructional quality and really effective teachers are therefore not considered effective, then those teachers are likely to alter the excellent instruction they've been providing. After all, everyone likes to be seen as successful. Thus, in schools where disadvantaged students don't earn sufficiently high scores on NCLB tests to avoid AYP failure, some desperate teachers will turn to excessive test-preparation drills. Students who were previously taught effectively will be forced to take part in mind-numbing test-prep sessions that at best end up enabling those students to answer a few more test items correctly. Yet, those hyper-drilled students' mastery of the essential features of what's been taught will often not have been boosted one bit.

Some teachers in schools where students don't score well on NCLB tests will often give no instructional attention to any content, even important content, that seems unlikely to be tested. "Why teach something," they conclude, "if it's not going to be on the accountability test?" Students in such classes are, thus, curricularly shortchanged. And this kind of curricular reductionism occurs chiefly because teachers in that school have been inaccurately identified as ineffective.

Such instructional sins as excessive test preparation or curricular reductionism can have long-lasting effects on the students being taught in a low-scoring, incorrectly evaluated school. But, as suggested, I'm every bit as dismayed about the potentially ineffective instruction received by students in affluent schools—schools everyone believes are successful. What may be going on in a school serving affluent students is simply that kids, regardless of how well they've been taught, are scoring well on their state's accountability tests. What's frightening about this is that some seriously shabby instruction may be taking place in many of our suburban schools—shabby instruction that fails to realize the considerable potential of those children. Yet, no one ever shrieks in dismay at this unfulfilled potential. Students are seen to be in "good schools" because these students score well on annual accountability tests. But those kids in good schools often could have been taught so much better. If only the public could realize that, in many but certainly not all instances, the instruction provided to students in our most affluent schools is in desperate need of improvement.

I hope it's clear how imperative it is that an educational accountability test be capable of distinguishing between effectively and ineffectively taught students. America's test-based educational accountability is fatally flawed if the tests can't do that. Regrettably, I believe the vast majority of the educational accountability tests now used are instructionally

SIDEBAR 5.1

Dipping Into—and Out of—Test Development

For about a decade, I directed an educational test–development company. Let me tell you how I got into, and why I got out of, the test-development game.

By the time the early seventies arrived, I had written several articles and two books about criterion-referenced measurement. When you write that much about something, people think you know what you are writing about. Sometimes you do.

Criterion-referenced measurement is an approach to testing based on how well the test-taker has mastered a well-defined criterion behavior, such as a cognitive skill or a body of knowledge. In contrast, norm-referenced measurement allows for the interpretation of a test-taker's score based on those of previous test-takers—the norm group—so that we can say, for example, "Molly scored at the 84th percentile, while Billy scored at the 49th percentile." Norm-referenced measurement strategies are employed in all of the nationally standardized achievement tests used in the U.S.

Back in those years, I had been arguing in what I wrote about criterion-referenced assessment that educational test–development firms ought to be producing more tests based on a criterion-referenced approach and fewer tests using a norm-referenced model. My pleas were not heeded. So, in the mid-seventies, I decided that a small company I then directed should get into the business of developing criterion-referenced tests. I was running this little outfit, IOX, in whatever spare time I had from my UCLA faculty responsibilities. This meant I was doing a lot of weekend, early morning, and late-night work at IOX.

At its largest, IOX had about thirty-five employees and we ended up building large-scale assessments for about a dozen states, often bidding for such work against much larger testing companies. In most projects we undertook, we would build the tests ourselves but would hire subcontractors to score and report students' test performances. What I found exciting about my moonlighting job was that almost all of the tests we created were designed to improve a state's instruction. For example, the first state test we developed was in 1979 for South Carolina, and the criterion-referenced approach we employed focused on measuring a modest number of significant, well-described skills in reading, writing, and mathematics. Our tests, then, measured students' achievement of those skills so that South Carolina's teachers could discern which skills were causing students trouble and which ones had been mastered. Because teachers were far too familiar with norm-referenced tests that provided little in the way of diagnostic information, I was delighted to see so many appreciating the instructional orientation of the tests we were producing, first in South Carolina and, thereafter, in other states.

But after about a decade of creating such tests, I decided it was time to exit that field—and hurriedly. As I noted above, when we bid on most test-development contracts, we invariably went head-to-head against some of the nation's largest testing companies. And we often beat them! Those were delicious victories, and I sometimes felt like David playing in Goliath's sandbox under his nose. But then, after about ten years, the sandbox rules suddenly shifted.

In the past, we would bid on a test-development request for proposals (RFP) issued by a state if we thought we could build the tests needed. Although we tried to keep our costs down, we were never the lowest priced company to respond to an RFP. IOX staff members included more than thirty smart and verbally astute professionals and, in Los Angeles especially, smart and verbally astute professionals expect to earn decent salaries. So, more often than not, our proposed contract would come in about the middle of the pack of potential bidders. Even so, we often ended up as the winning contractor.

However, in the late eighties, we found that we were suddenly bidding against large testing companies that had submitted a bid of no cost—that is, no cost whatsoever to the state that had issued the RFP. These large firms could submit no-cost proposals because they realized they would be able to more than make up for the lost development dollars by selling peripheral products—that is, a variety of tests for grades in which no testing was required—but tests that might be purchased by local school districts. Test-related instructional materials could also be sold in states where a well-known test was being used. In short, these no-cost bidders had ways of overcoming what was a variant of a "loss leader" test-development strategy where you sell one product well below cost, then make it up on the sale of other products.

Our little company definitely did not have the array of peripheral products that would allow us to compete against this strategy, so after three successive failures in bidding on state test-development projects—losing each time (and understandably) to a no-cost bid from a competitor—I realized it was time to move to more pleasant pastures. We downsized dramatically—essentially to near nonexistence.

What I learned from those ten years of test-development work is that, if state officials set out to adopt a criterion-referenced assessment strategy to

continued

SIDEBAR 5.1 *continued*

build their important tests and deliberately attempt to create tests that help improve instruction in their state, this can be done. Happily, those same instruction-oriented tests can be constructed so they help accurately evaluate instructional quality in the state's schools and districts. I know this can be done because I have seen it done first-hand.

Based on those ten years, however, I can now be accurately identified as a recovering test developer. Since the early nineties, I have been following an excellent twelve-step recovery program. It seems to be working.

---

insensitive. If I'm right, then not only are thousands of schools being inaccurately evaluated but—far worse—millions of our students are being educated less well than they should be.

Let's take a closer look at the concept at the heart of this particular educational mistake, namely, instructional sensitivity. I contend that since educational accountability began in this nation, educators have allowed their effectiveness to be measured with the wrong measuring sticks. Talk about an unlearned lesson!

INSTRUCTIONAL SENSITIVITY OF TESTS

Let's start off with a definition of instructional sensitivity:

> A test's instructional sensitivity represents the degree to which students' performances on that test accurately reflect the quality of instruction specifically provided to promote students' mastery of whatever is being assessed.

What this definition is saying is that a test is instructionally sensitive if effectively taught kids perform better than ineffectively taught kids. Conversely, a test is instructionally *in*sensitive if instructional quality has no impact on kids' test performance or, of course, if poorly taught kids score better than well-taught kids.

It is widely but wrongly believed that all accountability tests are instructionally sensitive. After all, many people think, this is why accountability tests were built in the first place. What I hope to show is why that thinking is flawed. Let's get under way by seeing, in rapid-rewind fashion, how we arrived at today's sorry situation with respect to the instructional insensitivity of our nation's accountability tests.

World War I and comparative score interpretations

In the early days of World War I, the U.S. Army was encountering considerable difficulty in identifying recruits who should be sent to officer training programs. The U.S. had never taken part in a war of this magnitude, and military officials simply didn't know how to spot those men who were likely to become suitable officers. Faced with this dilemma, Army officials turned to the American Psychological Association and its president, Robert Yerkes, who soon assembled a committee in late May, 1917, at the Vineland Training School in Vineland, New Jersey. In seven days, this committee created the Army Alpha, a group-administered test containing quantitative and verbal items intended to measure a recruit's intelligence.

The Alpha, which was administered to more than 1,700,000 men during WWI, represented the first large-scale use of group intelligence tests, and it was enormously successful. Scores were interpreted comparatively; that is, a recruit scored at the 96th percentile by outperforming 96 percent of a group of previous Alpha test-takers. These comparative interpretations proved highly useful to the military establishment in deciding which recruits to assign to officer training programs. The Alpha was an aptitude test, and examinees' scores were considered to represent their innate potential and readiness to learn—that is, their aptitude for becoming an officer. Given the many statistical analyses that were carried out to ensure the Alpha's technical quality and the Army's almost complete satisfaction with the test, it is not surprising that the comparative assessment strategy embodied in the Army Alpha was adopted by other test developers.

For example, in 1923, a few years after World War I ended, the initial versions of the Stanford Achievement Tests were published. (The Stanford is one of the nation's most popular standardized achievement tests and is currently in its tenth edition.) Even though the measurement mission of many of these post–World War I achievement tests was decidedly different than the mission of the Alpha, these successor tests all adopted the "proven" comparative-assessment strategy embodied in the predictor tests used by the Army. Achievement tests, for instance, are supposed to measure how much a student knows, for example, his or her reading ability or depth of historical knowledge. Aptitude tests, in contrast, are intended to detect differences among test-takers so that predictions can be made regarding a candidate's future success in some subsequent setting (such as an officer training program).

The Army Alpha's considerable success unfortunately made it the model for many subsequent achievement tests. An almost slavish emulation of the Alpha's assessment approach occurred, even though a comparative strategy for measuring students' achievement often turned out to be misleading. To this day, many accountability tests used in the U.S. have been created with an Army Alpha measurement mission in mind, namely, the comparison of test-takers. As you will see, this assessment approach almost certainly diminishes the instructional sensitivity of an educational accountability test.

Traditional standardized achievement tests

Roughly half of the state-level accountability tests currently used in the U.S. are nationally standardized achievement tests, such as the Stanford or the Iowa Tests of Basic Skills. Typically, a state's officials choose one of these off-the-shelf national tests to serve as its annual accountability test, then oblige the company that sells the test to add some items, so that the resultant "augmented" test will mesh better with that state's particular curricular aims. But even these augmented versions of traditional standardized achievement tests suffer from the same shortcoming as their un-augmented predecessors—they still are governed by an Alpha-like comparative measurement mission.

That's right, the rationale underlying all commercially developed, nationally standardized achievement tests is to provide scores from which accurate comparisons can be made. To do so, especially considering the brief amount of time in which the tests must be administered (typically about an hour), it is crucial for a standardized achievement test to produce ample score spread so there will be substantial differences among the test-takers' scores.

To use an extreme—and silly—example, if all of the students who completed a particular standardized achievement test earned the identical overall score, it would be literally impossible to compare them. Thus, what the people who create standardized tests yearn for is substantial spread in students' scores—the more spread the better. If test-takers' scores are well distributed, with lots of middling scores and, at least, a meaningful number of high scores and low scores, then the test will almost certainly perform its comparative measurement mission successfully.

But how do the creators of standardized achievement tests make certain their tests generate sufficient score spread? Well, in a nutshell, these test-developers make sure their tests contain plenty of items that do a good job of spreading out test-takers' scores. What this means in practical terms is that standardized achievement tests should predominantly consist of items that will be answered correctly by only about half of the test-takers—between, say, 40 percent and 60 percent of those who take the test. Statistically speaking, a test item that's answered correctly by only half of the examinees maximizes its contribution to the overall test's score spread. In fact, these items are cherished by those who build standardized achievement tests.

We refer to the percentage of students who answer a particular test item correctly as the item's p-value. Too many items with a high p-value (for example, $p = .95$ or $p = .89$) or too many items with a low p-value (for example, $p = .12$ or $p = .21$) would substantially reduce a test's likelihood of producing sufficient score spread to permit the fine-grained comparisons necessary for this sort of assessment. Traditionally constructed standardized achievement tests need to make it possible for test users to distinguish between students who score at, say, the 86th percentile and those who score at the adjacent percentiles, the 85th and 87th.

Many people think of an item's p-value as an indication of the item's difficulty. Items with low p-values (say, below .20) are often regarded as tough, while items with high p-values (say, above .80) are thought to be easy. But this perception, popular as it is, just isn't accurate. Students' performance on a given test item reflects not only the inherent difficulty of that item's content but also how well students have been taught whatever the item is measuring. Regarding an item's inherent difficulty, it is apparent that asking a child to multiply 949 times 673 is more demanding than asking the child to multiply 11 times 2. But the way students perform on an item also depends how well they were taught. To illustrate this point, if a teacher in an advanced physics class does a crackerjack job of teaching students to understand a complicated principle of quantum physics, most of the items on the final exam that are based on this abstruse principle might end up having *p*-values of .90 or higher. After all, the test-takers were taught well about this complicated principle. However, if those same test items are given to other, equally bright students who never studied advanced physics, the *p*-values for those other students might hover around zero.

What the folks who construct traditional standardized achievement tests want, therefore, are test items that will contribute to score spread, even if many teachers did a superb job of instructing what's being assessed. In a perverse way, because too many well-taught students would clearly diminish a standardized achievement test's ability to compare test-takers accurately, such tests would do a better job if they were not sensitive to instruction. I'm not claiming that the developers of traditional standardized achievement tests set out to make their tests insensitive to instruction, but I do believe they make little effort to enhance the instructional sensitivity of their test items.

There are two types of test items almost certain to produce score spread: items linked to students' socioeconomic status (SES) and items linked to students' inherited academic aptitudes.

SES-Linked Items. Students whose parents are well educated and have high earnings are regarded as high-SES students. Because SES is a nicely spread-out variable and one that isn't altered rapidly, if students' answers to a test item are apt to be influenced by their family's SES, then the item is almost certain to produce its share of score spread. Consider, for example, the following item from a nationally standardized achievement test in science, a test designed for middle school students:

A Middle School Science Item
Because a plant's fruit invariably contains seeds, which of the following is *not* a fruit?
- a. Apple
- b. Pumpkin
- c. Orange
- *d. Celery

As the asterisk indicates, the correct answer is D. Incidentally, I've altered the item only slightly (without changing the essence of what it is trying to measure) from an actual item that appears in a current national standardized achievement test. This item, however, is clearly linked to SES. Students from high-SES families are likely to do better on this item than their low-SES classmates. If you're a high-SES kid, odds are that your parents have purchased fresh celery (that is, seedless fresh celery) from the local supermarket. You're also likely to have had fresh pumpkins for carving jack-o-lanterns on Halloween, so you'd know that any self-respecting pumpkin is always filled with a swarm of pumpkin seeds. If you are a low-SES kid for whom fresh produce is a luxury, you may never have encountered a stalk of celery face-to-face.

Will all high-SES kids answer this item correctly and all low-SES kids miss it? Of course not. But if we were to administer the item to one hundred randomly selected low-SES and one hundred high-SES middle school students, I'll bet a lifetime supply of seed-free celery that more of the high-SES kids will come up with the right answer. This sort of probabilistic edge, perhaps only a slight one, is all that's needed for items on traditionally constructed standardized achievement tests to accomplish their measurement mission. Yet, the degree to which students' SES status is influencing their performance on an item—even if that influence is subtle—reduces that item's ability to measure how well the students were taught. If there are many SES-linked items on a standardized test, then the test's instructional sensitivity is reduced accordingly. SES-linked items measure what students bring to school, not what students are taught at school.

Items Linked to Students' Inherited Academic Aptitudes. Students are born with dissimilar levels of academic aptitude such as their verbal, quantitative, or spatial aptitudes. Howard Gardner posits the existence of numerous kinds of intelligences, three of which are often linked to the items that make up traditional standardized achievement tests.[2] Students, depending on how fortunate they were when their personal gene-pool lottery took place, differ in how easily they deal with verbal, quantitative, or spatial problems. Some kids *genetically* find it easier to deal with, say, verbal or spatial problems. I should emphasize that if a student is born with only moderate quantitative aptitude, this definitely does not preclude this student's attaining a high level of prowess in mathematics. However, it may be more difficult and take much longer for such students to become accomplished in mathematics.

Just as we saw with SES, there is a spread among students' innate academic aptitudes. The spread of inherited aptitudes means that an aptitude-linked item can produce the kind of score spreading so necessary for achievement tests, which in many ways are simply today's incarnations of the Army Alpha exams.

Aptitude-linked items are related to a nicely spread out variable, students' inherited academic aptitudes, and as was true with SES, this variable doesn't change all that rapidly. Accordingly, aptitude-linked items do a super job of producing the much-needed score spread sought by the architects of traditional standardized achievement tests. It is not surprising, then, that in most of these tests we find a flock of items closely linked to students' inherited verbal, quantitative, and spatial aptitudes.

Below is another item drawn from a current national standardized achievement test, this one from a middle school social studies exam.

A Middle-School Social Studies Item

If your family seriously wants to "go green" by conserving natural resources, which one of these actions would be most effective for you to use in this effort?

   a. Frequently washing small loads in a washing machine instead of washing large loads less often.

*b. Completing homework assignments by, whenever possible, writing on both sides of a piece of paper.

   c. Leaving lights on in a house or apartment even if they are not needed.

   d. Placing all used plastic bottles and used newspapers immediately into trash containers.

A student with strong verbal aptitude will have a better chance of coming up with a correct answer to this item, regardless of how much he or she has been taught about conservation. This is because a verbally able student (a "word smart" student, using Gardner's label) will figure out that the correct answer to the item depends on determining which of the four actions will best contribute to "conserving natural resources."

Once the test-taker has sorted out the verbal thrust of the item, it is a fairly straightforward task to identify which choice is, in fact, most likely to save natural resources.

Just as we saw with SES-linked items, students' inherited academic aptitudes are spread out well and don't change all that rapidly. As a consequence, an achievement test that's loaded with aptitude-linked items is certain to create the cherished score spread on which these tests are predicated. But items assessing students' inherited academic aptitudes, as was true with SES-linked items, typically measure what students bring to school, not what they're taught once they arrive.

So, if a state's accountability test is fashioned along the lines of a traditional nationally standardized achievement test, it is almost certain the test will be less instructionally sensitive than it should be. And this is true whether or not the test has been "augmented" with items more closely aligned with state content standards that were not well addressed in the "off-the-shelf" test. But, as indicated earlier, only about half of state-level accountability tests are traditional standardized achievement tests. What about the rest? Let's see.

Customized standards-based accountability tests

The other half of the state-level accountability tests used in the U.S. are custom-built, standards-based examinations. The typical assessment approach used for these accountability tests is that state officials hire an external test-development agency (one of a half-dozen or so large assessment firms) to build a test that measures students' mastery of the state's official content standards—that is, the curricular aims describing the skills and knowledge the state's students are supposed to learn. It is for the reason that these tests assess students' mastery of those content standards; such tests are characterized as "standards-based" exams.

This assessment strategy might seem to represent an eminently sensible way to build accountability tests—that is, identify the stuff we want kids to learn, then build tests to determine whether, in fact, they learned it. But many state education officials blundered when they set forth the content standards they wanted a state's students to learn. They committed the first of the six mistakes described in this book and ended up with a *wish list* of far too many curricular aims—far too many to teach, far too many to test.

Given what sometimes turned out to be literally hundreds of curricular aims to measure, the assessment firms that were hired to create standards-based accountability tests did really the only thing they could. Because of the limited time available to assess students' status relative to the entire array of a state's curricular targets, most of the firms building these tests adopted the solution of sampling from the too-many targets. It was, realistically, about the only strategy they could adopt. Thus, having too many targets to assess and too little time to assess them translated into an approach wherein state accountability tests measured only some—not all—of the curricular targets eligible to be assessed each year. Occasionally a curricular aim was measured with a few items, sometimes it was measured with one item, and sometimes it was not measured at all.

Predictably, this unpredictable sampling-based approach to accountability testing meant that state educators were obliged to guess which curricular aims would be assessed each year. Sometimes teachers guessed well, often they didn't. As a consequence of this guessing-game approach to preparing students for accountability exams, many teachers ended up emphasizing curricular aims that weren't measured on those exams and failing to emphasize those that were actually measured. Off-target teaching was the rule, not the exception.

After a few frustrating years of off-target teaching, many teachers in states where customized standards-based tests were used simply gave up trying to out-guess which of the myriad curricular aims were going to be assessed in the approaching accountability tests. And once teachers began giving only perfunctory instructional attention to the pursuit of content standards, guess which factors end up being most influential in determining students' scores on standards-based accountability tests? If you guessed students' socioeconomic status and inherited academic aptitudes, you are absolutely correct.

That's right. These are the same two factors that played such a potent role in determining how well students were likely to score on traditional standardized achievement tests. And just as we saw with these tests, students' scores on standards-based tests tend to measure what students bring to school—their socioeconomic status and innate academic aptitude—rather than what they are taught in school. For an accountability test to be truly sensitive to instruction, it must measure how well students have been taught.

A CONTINUUM

Few if any accountability tests are totally sensitive or totally insensitive to instruction. Some tests surely do a better job of determining how well students have been taught. It makes less sense to think of instructional sensitivity as an on/off variable and instead to regard it as the sort of continuum seen in figure 5.1. If an accountability test contains many SES-linked or aptitude-linked items, it is more likely to be classified near the insensitivity end of a continuum. Conversely, if there are few such items on a test, it might be near the high end of the continuum.

In late 2001, I reported the results of a personal analysis of several traditional national standardized achievement tests currently in use. I had undertaken an item-by-item review of the tests in which I attempted—as objectively as possible—to determine what percentage of their items were linked to either SES or aptitude.[3] These results are summarized in table 5.1.

If you consider the percentage of items that I concluded were linked to either SES or aptitude (and, of course, sometimes an item was linked to both), it should be clear that we are not dealing with a trifling problem. If I (or anyone else) took a serious item-by-item gander at any of today's accountability exams, I submit that the results of such an analysis would parallel those I reported several years ago.

I was as careful as I could be in judging these items but, just for argument's sake, let's say I was too stringent in my scrutiny. Let's say, in fact,

FIGURE 5.1 *A Continuum of Instructional Sensitivity for Educational Accountability Tests*

TABLE 5.1 *Percentages of Nationally Standardized Achievement Test Items Judged to be Linked to Students' Socioeconomic Status (SES) or their Inherited Academic Aptitudes*

Subject	SES-Linked Item Percentage	Aptitude-Linked Item Percentage
Reading	15	40
Language Arts	65	35
Mathematics	5	20
Science	45	55
Social Studies	45	50

that I was twice as tough as I should have been and chop all my percentages right down the middle. My point is that if you were to take only half of the percentages seen in table 5.1, there would still be way too many items that might diminish the instructional sensitivity of an accountability test.

Remember, whenever an educational accountability test—whether a traditional standardized achievement test or a customized standards-based test—is seriously insensitive to instruction, two bad things happen: schools are inaccurately evaluated, and desperate teachers adopt classroom practices that are educationally harmful to students. Neither of those should be allowed to happen.

Who's at fault here?

For at least the last several decades, a test-based educational accountability movement has been taking shape in America, a movement that emerged from doubts about the quality of our schools—doubts that surely have not subsided. Yet I have been arguing that the cornerstone tools of this accountability juggernaut—namely, its accountability tests—are unable to accurately distinguish between good and bad instruction. Is this not the essence of absurdity? And who, pray tell, is at fault for allowing this silliness to go on for as long as it has?

My answer may not please you, but it's the answer I think is accurate. I believe those most fundamentally at fault for letting this happen are educational professionals. Too many of us sat back meekly while a grossly inappropriate collection of measurement tools was used to determine how effective we were. It was our gaffe—no one else's. But it is a reversible mistake, as I hope you'll recognize.

Looking back, just as soon as educational policymakers, whether at the state, local, or federal level, began to judge the quality of education based on students' test performance, we should have been all over those tests like flies on spoiled fruit, making dead certain that those assessments were appropriate for this sort of evaluative application.

It's not that I'm opposed to the use of accountability tests as a powerful, perhaps the most powerful, way of getting evidence about educational quality. I'd certainly want to see other credible evidence tossed into the evaluative hopper, but using tests of students' achievement to make sure those students have been well taught makes scads of sense to me. Yes, those tests should be standardized, but the right kinds of tests—instructionally sensitive ones—must be employed. If we use the wrong tests, we'll end up with the wrong results.

So why did the education profession sit calmly on its collective duff while outrageously inappropriate accountability tests were installed in state after state? The answer is obvious: America's educators allowed themselves to be evaluated with fundamentally flawed accountability tests because of one thing—a huge lump of ignorance.

American educators were essentially ignorant about educational tests and they assumed the right kinds of tests would be chosen for this important job. But they never checked whether this crucial assumption was warranted. One reason educators were reluctant to judge the suitability of accountability tests is that few of them knew very much about even the basics of educational assessment. Until recently, teachers and administrators have not been extensively trained in educational assessment, and the field of measurement is often regarded as intimidating—as too quantitative and esoteric for most. As a consequence, few educators were in a position to question the decisions that brought to their state a set of accountability tests unable to accurately measure educators' success. Unfortunately, this ignorance regarding educational assessment is still prevalent among the nation's educators (as will be addressed in the next chapter).

But we have now seen the fruits of this assessment acquiescence. We have now seen that as long as the wrong kinds of educational accountability tests are in place, the wrong kinds of evaluative conclusions will be reached. This is a mistake, therefore, that must be corrected—immediately.

A LESSON-LEARNT SOLUTION

As long as we're dealing with a mistake related to educational measurement, there's an analogous situation where a successful two-pronged solution to an assessment problem begs to be emulated. Let's look, briefly, at what was done during the last couple of decades to rectify a prominent measurement shortcoming, namely, assessment bias.

Borrowing from bias detection

The current circumstances in state-level accountability testing are strikingly similar to the assessment situation in the U.S. only a few decades ago with respect to assessment bias. At that time, although most measurement specialists knew what was meant when assessment bias was discussed, there was rarely any systematic effort during the construction of major educational tests to identify and eliminate items apt to offend or unfairly penalize test-takers on the basis of personal characteristics such as race, gender, or ethnicity. As a result, many test-based inferences about certain groups of students were made with less validity than those inferences should have been.

But then the measurement community set out to devise ways of gauging assessment bias and, within a relatively few years, educational tests became markedly less biased. Once the bias-detection tools were in place, educators quite properly demanded that they be used in the most important educational assessments.

The two strategies for detecting assessment bias were rooted in judgmental and empirical procedures. Judgmentally, we trained experienced educators—who typically represented all the subgroups of test-takers apt to be affected adversely by test bias—to review items, one at a time, in an effort to detect elements that might offend or unfairly penalize examinees. Empirically, we compared the performance levels of majority and minority subgroups on each item in a test to see if, for instance, majority test-takers dramatically outperformed minority test-takers. In the early days of assessment-bias detection, these contrasts consisted of little more than a comparison of the proportions of different subgroups who had answered each item correctly (an item's p-value). Later, as more sophisticated bias-detection procedures evolved, great reliance was placed on "differential item functioning," wherein analyses attempted to discern whether an item appeared to function differently for two dissimilar subgroups. When these two general strategies (empirical and judgmental) were used in concert, a potent bias-eradication approach allowed assessment personnel to meaningfully reduce the number of biased items in their tests.

There is no reason we should not employ precisely the same two-pronged approach in determining a test's instructional sensitivity. Happily, what we have learned from the past generation's efforts to reduce assessment bias is that these procedures need be neither inordinately expensive nor excessively time-consuming. The more routine and cost effective we can make instructional sensitivity detection procedures, the more likely it is these procedures will be used. Moreover, the more frequently instructional sensitivity detection procedures are used, the more instructionally sensitive a state's accountability tests are likely to be. And, finally, the more instructionally sensitive a state's educational accountability tests are, the less likely it is that these assessments will trigger instructionally harmful practices and misleading evaluations of educators' successes or failures. Such shortcomings will be reduced simply because the state's assessments have been made more accurate and, as a consequence, more fair to educators.

Judgmental analysis

One approach to the detection of instructional sensitivity requires little expenditure of energy. All it involves is the inclusion of an additional quality criterion, to be used whenever items under development are being scrutinized. In most states, this scrutiny takes place before field testing of test items, for example, during reviews of the test items' alignment with curricular aims or, perhaps, during a review to detect whether any items are biased. Reviewers could be asked to answer a question about each potential item; for example, "If a teacher has provided reasonably effective instruction directed toward the curricular aim this item is supposed to measure [the particular curricular aim would be identified], is it likely the bulk of that teacher's students will answer this item correctly?"

The group of reviewers asked to evaluate this item could easily be given an orientation regarding how to evaluate instructional sensitivity, and per-item data could be routinely collected so that after gaining sufficient experience, the state's assessment staff would be able to identify items they consider too instructionally insensitive to be used. Clearly, this sort of review would lead external assessment contractors to become more attentive to this dimension of quality when constructing new items.

From the perspective of state assessment personnel, giving judgmentally focused attention to instructional sensitivity would seem to require only a modest elaboration of the review procedures that are already in place.

Empirical analysis

In addition to judgmental approaches to detecting instructional sensitivity, it is also possible to employ empirical procedures to determine whether individual test items are sufficiently sensitive to instruction. Because empirical strategies require the actual administration and scoring of test items, empirical approaches to determining instructional sensitivity almost always involve a higher level of commitment and energy than would be required for a judgmental approach. Nonetheless, if efficient and cost-effective methods of empirically ascertaining the instructional sensitivity of test items can be devised, those methods can be a useful adjunct to conclusions based on judgmental strategies. At the very least, the occasional use of empirical procedures to confirm the accuracy of judgmental review methods would be beneficial.

In essence, empirical methods of determining the instructional sensitivity of test items boil down to contrasting the performance of effectively and ineffectively taught students. Thus, if students' performance on an item designed to measure a certain body of material is the same regardless of how effectively they have been taught this material, that item is instructionally insensitive.

Although there are important methodological considerations that must be attended to in order to arrive at such comparisons, this is the heart of what's involved in an empirical procedure for ascertaining the instructional sensitivity of accountability test items.

Realistically, it is almost impossible to locate two comparable groups of students, one that has been taught to master a particular skill or body of knowledge and one that hasn't. This is because most teachers are supposed to promote students' mastery of the same curricular aims at about the same time during the school year. Accordingly, it makes more methodological sense to compare the performance of students who have been taught a particular curricular aim effectively, rather than not effectively. But how can we find out which of the curricular aims measured by an accountability test have been taught more effectively and which less effectively? The simple answer is that we ask teachers.

It may seem laughable to ask teachers to identify the quality of their teaching of particular curricular aims, but is it? I believe that by carefully crafting self-report inventories—inventories that require teachers to identify themselves—we can minimize the likelihood of teachers' supplying socially desirable responses. Remember, the mission of any instructional-sensitivity inquiry is to render an accountability test more accurate and, as a consequence, more fair to teachers. Once teachers understand why they are being asked to supply estimates of their own instructional effectiveness, most will be willing to supply candid responses—even with the knowledge that their responses are identifiable. The challenge is to devise self-report surveys that do not threaten the teachers who are being asked to complete them.

One procedure for doing this is to ask teachers to consider the complete set of curricular aims that are eligible to be assessed on an accountability test, then divide those aims into three approximately equal groups according to the relative effectiveness with which the teacher taught them. The self-report survey must make clear there is no implication that the responding teacher did not teach every curricular aim satisfactorily. Indeed, all of the curricular aims under consideration might have been taught marvelously. Teachers will simply be asked to identify their most effectively taught and their least effectively taught curricular aims. But, before they are asked to complete such a survey, all prospective respondents must be thoroughly apprised of why they are being asked to report—in any way at all—about their instructional effectiveness. If teachers do not understand clearly why they are being surveyed, we cannot expect them to participate forthrightly in this data-gathering effort.

But Are They Willing?

In attempting to collect evidence about whether test items can distinguish between well-taught and not-so-well-taught students, there are basically two ways to proceed: judgmentally and empirically. Judgmentally, we can review all items under development that will possibly be used on an accountability test, one item at a time. We do this by asking seasoned educators to judge whether an item seems likely to differentiate among students according to how well they have been taught. Empirically, however, we need to contrast students' actual test performance—again, item by item—to see whether well-taught students actually out perform students who have not been taught as well. To carry out such empirical analyses, we need to ask teachers to supply information about their own teaching that might be threatening to them. The question, then, is whether teachers would be willing to supply potentially "self-incriminating" evidence of their own teaching.

Well, educational officials in the Mississippi Department of Education (MDE) decided to determine whether teachers in their state would be willing to supply judgments about the quality of their own teaching—judgments that might be used against them. I believe you'll be interested in what we discovered in Mississippi.

Two MDE education officials led the inquiry: Kristopher Kaase, the state's assistant superintendent, and Cindy Simmons, the state's assessment director. In an attempt to study the instructional sensitivity of their state's accountability tests, in 2008 Kris and Cindy carried out several small-scale studies with Mississippi teachers to see if they would be willing to supply information about their personal instructional effectiveness. Here's how the studies unfolded.

To begin with, several separate groups of a dozen or so teachers were informed that the only rationale for these studies was to increase the fairness of all MDE accountability tests. Teachers were also assured, in writing, that the results of the study would never be used to evaluate the quality of any Mississippi teacher. Next, the teachers were asked if they would be willing to complete a rating form dealing with the entire set of state-approved (and state-assessed) objectives that Mississippi teachers were to promote for their students, first in language arts and, thereafter, in mathematics. On the rating forms, teachers were asked to identify the one-third of the objectives in each subject that they had taught "most successfully" and the one-third they had taught "least successfully." For instance, if there were twelve objectives to be taught (and tested) in language arts, the teachers would identify their four best-taught and four worst-taught objectives. It was emphasized that this did not in any way imply that all of the objectives in a given subject had not been taught wonderfully. What a teacher's ratings were to indicate, however, was whether some objectives had been taught more wonderfully than others.

Teachers were asked to supply their names on the rating forms because, after students had completed the state accountability tests, their performance on the items measuring each objective would be compared according to which teacher taught which students. More specifically, the item-by-item performance of "more successfully taught" students (those whose teachers indicated that a particular objective was one of their best taught) would be contrasted with the performances of "least successfully taught" students (those whose teachers indicated that a particular objective was one of their worst taught). If an item measuring a particular objective was answered correctly more often by best-taught students than by worst-taught students, then the item would be regarded as instructionally sensitive. If not, then the item would be deemed to be instructionally insensitive. However, because the analysis of students' per-item performance would have to be based on how well a student's own teacher thought particular objectives had been taught, teachers had to identify themselves on their rating forms.

In June 2008, Kris, Cindy, and I spent several days with different groups of teachers in Jackson, Mississippi, explaining the nature of the rating tasks and finding out whether the teachers would be willing to rank the relative effectiveness of their teaching relative to the objectives being measured by MDE accountability tests. We were, quite frankly, unsure whether teachers would be willing to do what were asking.

To our surprise and delight, all the participating teachers indicated a willingness to sign their names on the rating forms in which they signified their comparative success in promoting students' mastery of the objectives measured by MDE accountability tests. What they wanted more than anything else, it seems, were accountability tests that would accurately and fairly evaluate Mississippi teachers' effectiveness.

However, many of the teachers expressed concerns about whether they could, with sufficient accuracy, distinguish between their best-taught and worst-taught objectives. Several of the teachers offered excellent suggestions to MDE for helping teachers get a more accurate fix on which objectives had been most effectively or least effectively taught. One of those suggestions was

continued

SIDEBAR 3.1 *continued*

for the MDE to prepare a brief video to be played to the state's teachers early in the school year that laid out specific ways of gathering evidence throughout the year regarding which objectives had been best learned by students, hence best taught.

Are teachers willing to play this sort of "names-given" evaluative game to ensure the heightened instructional sensitivity of their state's accountability tests? It seems, at least in Mississippi, they are.

Teachers also must be assured that any data they supply will never be used to evaluate teachers, schools, or districts. The only purpose of asking teachers to identify their most successfully and least successfully taught curricular aims is to help state assessment personnel isolate items on accountability tests that may be insufficiently sensitive to instruction.

Once teachers have identified their most and least successfully taught curricular aims, then the students those teachers have just finished teaching are divided—one curricular aim at a time—into the students of teachers who thought they taught a curricular aim most successfully, and the students of teachers who thought they taught it least successfully. Using students' performances on a state's annual accountability text, a simple index of per-item instructional sensitivity can be calculated by subtracting the performance level on an item of ineffectively taught students from the performance level on that same item of effectively taught students. If this difference is positive and large, the item would appear to be instructionally sensitive. If the difference is nonexistent or negative, the item would appear to be instructionally insensitive. Clearly, different curricular aims would have different groups of students involved in the data analyses. The analysis of such data, however, should be relatively straightforward.

Urging state assessment officials to act

This lesson-learnt solution strategy boils down to a fairly simple approach, namely, pressure must be put on state education authorities so that the accountability tests they use to evaluate educators' efforts are fair to those educators in that they accurately determine instructional quality. If accountability tests are instructionally insensitive, they can't be used to evaluate instructional quality fairly or accurately. Only when those tests have been made as instructionally sensitive as possible will we be able to appropriately evaluate those who operate our schools. Without delay, this fifth mistake, this sadly unlearned lesson, needs to be remedied.

CHAPTER SIX

Abysmal Assessment Literacy

How would you feel if, upon becoming seriously ill, you were being treated by a doctor who didn't understand such medical fundamentals as the normal range of blood pressure, cholesterol, or blood sugar? If you weren't outraged by your physician's lack of familiarity with such basics, you should be.*

We expect professionals to possess a thoroughgoing mastery of the core concepts and procedures of their field. We assume, for instance, accountants should know that a balance sheet is not a nicely positioned piece of bed linen. And we expect that an attorney will definitely know that a tort is not a small pastry. Clearly, professionals are supposed to know the essential things about their specialties but, sadly, many educators don't.

Let's step back for just a moment to think about why we seek to educate children in the first place. There is, of course, the somewhat self-serving collective desire to ensure that our society long endures. Another of the main reasons we educate children is so they acquire the knowledge, skills, and affect they will need as adults. Let me focus for just a moment on that central mission, because it's one with which few people disagree.

---

*Certain sections of this chapter were adapted, with permission from the article, "Assessment Literacy for Teachers: Faddish or Fundamental?", I wrote for Volume 48, Issue 1 of *Theory into Practice* on the topic of classroom assessment. *TIP* is owned by The Ohio State University, College of Education and Human Ecology, and published by Taylor & Francis Journals.

To the extent that educators are trying to deal with students' knowledge, skills, and affect, we are dealing with the *unseen*. Teachers can't see how much knowledge a student has about the Civil War, or whether a student can extract square roots without a calculator, or even if a student is tolerant of those who hold different views of the world. Even with modern medical-imaging technology, we can't see what lurks inside students' heads.

How should educators cope with this conundrum? The answer, although it is not a perfectly reliable one, is for educators to assess a student's observable behavior (the student's responses to a test, for example) in order to make inferences about the student's *un*observable knowledge, skills, or affect. When a teacher sees that a student can correctly answer a flock of double-digit multiplication problems presented in a weekly test, the teacher *infers* that the student possesses the skill to multiply other such numbers. The use of tests, indeed, is the only practical way teachers have of figuring out what is going on inside their students' heads.

Accordingly, because tests are the chief tools teachers must use to determine whether their instruction actually works, we would expect that the nation's educators would be genuinely conversant with educational testing. But are they?

ANOTHER ERROR OF OMISSION

This book's sixth and final unlearned lesson is another error of omission. Put simply, most of today's educators know almost nothing about educational assessment. This harsh appraisal can be quickly confirmed by anyone who is willing to spend a few minutes interacting with just about any teachers or administrators who wander by in the faculty lounge. For many educators, "test" is a four-letter word, both literally and figuratively—an opaque and off-putting term.

This gaping hole in educators' assessment-related knowledge is not only all too apparent, it is all too understandable. The most obvious explanation for this is the correct one: when most of today's teachers completed their teacher-education programs and when most of today's administrators completed their administrator-training programs, they were not required to learn anything about educational assessment. So they didn't.

Most prospective teachers' days were crammed with all sorts of coursework and jammed with hours of obligatory time spent in public schools, first as observers and, later, as student teachers. Educators who were pursuing an administrative credential, frequently at the same time they were holding a full-time teaching job, also had little discretionary time. Given such temporal pressures, we can easily see why most prospective teachers and would-be administrators failed to enroll voluntarily in any nonrequired courses dealing with educational testing.

But it was more than insufficient time that deterred many of today's educators from completing courses in educational measurement. Sadly, many candidates for teacher or administrator credentials are intimidated by any content thought to be even mildly mathematical in nature. Far too many prospective teachers and administrators regard educational assessment as a quantitative cousin of the much dreaded subject to be avoided at any cost—educational statistics!

What I find so personally galling about the perceived quantitative moat surrounding the educational assessment castle is that it is absolutely unnecessary. What today's educators need to learn about the fundamentals of educational measurement need not require the use of any exotic numerical gyrations. What's truly important in educational assessment requires common sense, not esoteric mathematics. I fear that a few measurement specialists revel in rendering their field quantitatively intimidating because it keeps commoners out. Nevertheless, whether warranted or not, the reality is that many educators regard educational assessment as something too numerical for them to mess with. We need to correct that thoroughly mistaken perception.

Whatever the causes, current educators, other than having receiving a dollop of information in a preservice educational psychology class dealing with the care and feeding of test items, usually arrived at their first teaching assignment or showed up for their first administrative assignment quite bereft of any fundamental understanding of educational measurement. In recent years, fortunately, we have seen the emergence of increased preservice requirements that oblige some state's teacher-education candidates to acquire a grounding in educational assessment. But those requirements are far from universal. The situation with respect to the training of school administrators is much less positive. Few administrator-training programs in the U.S. now require administrative candidates to complete formal courses in educational assessment, perhaps because it is assumed, wrongly in most instances, that would-be administrators are already knowledgeable about the basics of educational measurement. So, for the nonce, if most of today's educators are going to acquire meaningful measurement moxie, it must be supplied in the form of professional development completed after teacher-education programs and administrative training.

Before proceeding, I need to set out the three assumptions the remainder of this chapter is guided by. The first is that the far too many of current classroom teachers and at least some school administrators truly do not know they need to possess a modicum of assessment knowledge, nor do they know what it is that they need to know about educational assessment. A second assumption is that this deficit situation can be rectified most realistically through professional development programs specifically aimed at the eradication of assessment literacy. A wrap-up assumption is that we need to get cracking without delay to make current educators' modest levels of assessment literacy an unpleasant but very distant memory.

Two types of assessment

If we could magically track a given teacher's total career in the classroom, minute-by-minute, we'd surely encounter innumerable instances in which educational assessment impinged directly on the decisions this teacher needed to make. Some of those assessment-related decisions would be quite important, such as whether a student should be promoted to the next grade. Some of them would be less important, such as whether the teacher should assign high or low en-route grades to students based on daily quizzes of trifling significance. It's fairly obvious that the seriousness of a teacher's assessment-related decisions can cover a substantial range. Similarly, some assessment-related decisions faced by school-based or district-level administrators will be really important, and some won't. So, granting that the significance of educators' assessment-related decisions can bounce all over the place, a key question remains: What kinds of assessments do educators most need to understand?

Currently, several sensible ways for educators to cut up their assessment cake are currently available. For instance, one increasingly popular distinction is to contrast summative assessment and formative assessment. As noted in chapter 2, summative assessment refers to the use of assessment-based evidence to make decisions about completed instructional events, such as the quality of an academic year's worth of schooling or the effectiveness of a semester-long algebra course. Summative assessment is intended to help arrive at go/no-go decisions based on the success of the final version of an instructional program. In contrast, formative assessment is a process in which assessment-elicited evidence is used by teachers to adjust their ongoing instructional activities or by students to adjust the ways they are trying to learn something. (Formative assessment, as you'll recall, was the focus of chapter 2.) In contrast to its summative sibling, formative assessment has a powerful improvement orientation because it is intended to generate needed adjustments in teachers' still malleable instructional programs or in students' current learning tactics.

Chiefly because of formative assessment's recent arrival on the measurement scene, the two kinds of assessments I use as a framework for this chapter are classroom assessments and accountability assessments. As noted several times earlier, the term "assessment" should be regarded not merely as a traditional paper-and-pencil test or, for that matter, as any kind of formal test. On the contrary, assessment consists of a wide variety of techniques used to elicit evidence, such as asking students to respond to teacher-presented questions by using white boards during a class discussion, conducting individual oral interviews with students, or systematically observing the interactions of students as they engage in collaborative problem-solving projects. Similarly, a school-level assessment of students' attitudes might use anonymous self-report inventories. To assess students' cognitive skills, teachers might employ an elaborate performance test on which students must complete, then describe in writing, a series of independent scientific experiments. Assessment, therefore, should definitely not be regarded as synonymous with test.

Classroom assessments refer to formal and informal procedures that teachers employ in an effort to make accurate inferences about what their students know and can do. Teachers sometimes use the results of classroom assessments to improve an instructional program already under way (especially if classroom formative assessment is in full flower). More often than not, unfortunately, the results of classroom assessments are used simply so teachers can dole out grades or perhaps use the prospect of an upcoming test to induce students to study harder. Although teachers generate most classroom assessments, they sometimes employ tests they find in a textbook or in the instructor's manuals accompanying their textbooks. Then, too, some districts—or even some state education departments—supply teachers with testing instruments or assessment procedures that teachers may, if they wish, employ as classroom assessments.

Accountability assessments, on the other hand, are measurement devices, almost always standardized, used by government entities such as states or school districts to determine the effectiveness of educational endeavors. In the U.S., the most prevalent accountability assessments are those required by NCLB, which calls for the annual administration of reading and mathematics accountability tests at several grade levels. Although officials of each state have a certain degree of autonomy in choosing the tests their state uses to satisfy NCLB assessment requirements, the federal government still exerts considerable pressure on states to use conventional testing instruments to satisfy U.S. Department of Education regulations and guidelines. A number of far-reaching decisions regarding schools and school districts are made according to students' performance on these accountability tests. To illustrate, if a particular school's staff is unable to improve its students' scores on state accountability tests for several successive years, the school's staff might be substantially restructured or the school might be closed down.

Two decision clusters

These days, there are two sets of assessment-related decisions that educators need to make. Not surprisingly, those decisions are linked to the two major categories, classroom assessment and accountability assessment. One set of decisions is related to teachers' day-to-day use of classroom assessments, such as which ones to employ and how the results should be used in class. But another, more subtle set of decisions stems from the nature of accountability tests, which, almost without exception, have a direct or indirect influence on what teachers do in their classrooms. Both sets of decisions have a meaningful impact on the way students end up being taught. Because assessment-literate educators will typically make better decisions than their colleagues who are basically baffled by assessment, and because we want students to be better educated, it should be obvious that today's educators should acquire substantially more assessment literacy—and the sooner the better.

Let's look first at classrooms assessments. If teachers are assessment literate, odds are that their classroom assessments will be better because those teachers will know not only what constitutes a defensible versus an indefensible assessment, but also what represents an accurate versus an inaccurate interpretation of assessment-elicited data. Classroom assessments, even if teachers use them in a fairly perfunctory fashion, will have at least some impact on the way students are educated. The more importance the teacher ascribes to classroom assessments, the more significant their impact will be on students' day-to-day instructional activities.

For example, suppose a teacher employs frequent classroom assessments as an integral part of a full-blown formative assessment strategy. It is clear that those assessments will play a prominent role in what goes on in the classroom. At the other extreme, even in a classroom where tests are used by a teacher only to assign grades or motivate students, flawed tests can soon discourage poorly assessed students, who in turn may find their academic motivation diminishing because their efforts are so unevenly rewarded. Less motivated students will, of course, usually end up being less well educated.

Classroom assessments, then, because their impact on the education process can range from modest to major, ought to be as good as possible. Teachers who are assessment literate will not only know how to create more suitable assessments, they will also be conversant with a wider array of assessment options than their less knowledgeable colleagues. Moreover, assessment-literate teachers who know the nuts and bolts of assessment will also understand how to spruce up the weaker items they created. The results of assessment ineptness should be expunged, and assessment-literate educators can do the expunging.

All teachers assess their students, some more intensively than others. Almost all assessments have an impact on instruction, some more substantially than others. Accordingly, all teachers need sufficient assessment literacy so their classroom assessments will be at least satisfactory, and preferably substantially better.

Administrators—both school-site and district-level administrators— can also have a major impact on the kinds of classroom assessments teachers employ. For instance, school principals can urge their faculties to employ a full range of assessment tactics and persuade them that assessments should come in flavors other than multiple-choice, true-false, or essays, but to do so the principal can't be an assessment ninny. Teachers will respect the assessment advice of administrators who clearly understand assessment, whereas administrators who lack such know-how and try to spout off about what teachers should be doing assessment-wise will usually receive the response they deserve. If an administrator's major mission is to ensure the quality of classroom instruction, then he or she must be sufficiently knowledgeable about the topic to give teachers the guidance they frequently need in order to use assessment in an instructionally supportive manner.

Turning now to accountability assessments, why do educators need assessment literacy to make decisions related to the use of such tests? As indicated above, although it is unarguable that both teachers and administrators need to be assessment literate insofar as such literacy bears on decisions related to classroom assessments, it is not immediately apparent why educators' assessment literacy is germane to the sorts of assessments traditionally used for accountability testing. After all, these are large-scale tests controlled by high-level governmental officials, not classroom teachers or school administrators. But, unfortunately, therein resides a fallacy that has flourished for far too long in America's schools.

Putting it candidly, U.S. educators have historically abdicated any role in controlling the nature of the assessment instruments that predominantly determine the perceived success of educators' instructional efforts. For members of any profession to allow—without serious scrutiny—their competence to be evaluated on the basis of assessment tools they have not thoroughly vetted is suicidal , but this is precisely what has gone on in the field of education for decades. Educators rarely, if ever, register their views regarding the quality of the accountability tests that are being employed to appraise their own competence, or fight for the opportunity to help decide whether a particular accountability test should actually be used. Nonetheless, what's past is, by definition, *past*. Educators, like all professionals, need to begin playing a pivotal role in deciding what sorts of assessments will be used to evaluate their competence.

A major reason educators are reluctant to scrutinize educational accountability tests is that most of them don't think they know enough to evaluate the quality of those tests. And they don't! The reason for this is that too many of them are not assessment literate. This needs to change.

You saw in the last chapter that most of the accountability tests now being used in the U.S. are instructionally insensitive, that is, they are unable to differentiate between effectively and ineffectively taught students. Well, because such accountability tests will yield a flawed picture of educators' instructional abilities, it is downright dimwitted for educators to allow themselves to be evaluated with these tools.

Accordingly, one key decision any educator should make regarding accountability tests is whether to try to replace or improve an inappropriate one. If the accountability test is okay, there's naught to be done. But few of today's accountability tests are okay, so an inappropriate test will usually need to be improved or replaced. Educators, whether separately, in small groups, or as part of a larger coalition, can decide whether to take aggressive action to educate, then influence, those who have installed unsound accountability tests. If educators can exercise the sort of leadership expected from enlightened professionals, then there's a chance that inadequate accountability assessments can in time be replaced by better ones. When our accountability assessments are instructionally sensitive, then our accountability programs will be able to work the way they are supposed to work, namely, to ensure that our students are on the receiving end of first-rate instruction.

Okay, I have suggested that when we split the world of educational testing into two lumps, classroom assessments and accountability assessments, educators will be faced with sets of decisions they ought to make about both. Both sets of decisions are important. Both sets of decisions have an impact on how students are educated. But, in order to make those decisions more defensibly, educators clearly need a solid dose of assessment literacy.

A QUICK CONTENT DIP

Professional development programs focused on assessment literacy need to be tailored. Although such programs designed for school administrators are likely to be similar to programs for teachers in that many of the topics to be treated would be essentially identical, some salient content differences would—and should—exist. I'd like to lay out the content

— p 135

SIDEBAR 6.1

Assessment Literacy in Perspective

In this chapter I have been chiding educators for their lack of assessment literacy. But, to be honest, for the early part of my own career I was a thoroughgoing assessment illiterate. I never took a course in educational measurement during my graduate student days, and it took me almost a decade to realize I had to start learning, on my own, about educational assessment. I am pleased to report that this self-study seemed to pay off, because in 2002 I received an award from an educational measurement association that both pleased and humbled me.

In New Orleans, on April 3, I received the 2002 Award for Career Contributions to Educational Measurement from the National Council on Educational Measurement. The award was made during the association's annual convention at the Wednesday breakfast meeting. It is an important award, and I was most pleased to have been chosen to receive it.

Later that day and into the evening, a large number of friends attending the meeting came up to me and offered their congratulations. I responded with the usual "Thank you" or some synonymous phrase. As I said, the Career Award is significant—and it even was accompanied by a hefty check—so I really was happy to receive it.

The next morning, because I cannot stand to pay $9 for a solitary muffin in the hotel lobby, I walked a half-block from the Marriott Hotel to Wendy's, where I purchased two egg sandwiches and a glass of orange juice for under $3. Happily basking in my thriftiness, I was about to dump my leftovers into a trash container when I spied an old, raggedy woman in a corner watching me. If she had been accompanied by a shopping cart, I would have concluded that she was a bag lady down on her luck . Well, she looked me straight in the eye for a moment and then said, "Congratulation!"

Although I instantly responded with a knee-jerk "Thank you," I really was perplexed. How on earth had this old woman learned of my award? Her attire suggested that she was not a regular attendee at national meetings of measurement associations. What was going on?

I suspect that my confusion was evident to her because, after a moment, she explained: "You're the first man today who's bussed his own tray."

And thus I learned that my measurement fame had not spread to the fast-food crowd. I returned to the conference a suitably sobered awardee.

that should be addressed—in a real-world, practical manner rather than in an esoteric, theoretical fashion—in a program for educators to develop assessment literacy. This will only be a list of potential content; those who are interested will find a more detailed treatment in other sources.[1]

- The fundamental function of educational assessment—namely, the collection of evidence from which inferences can be made about students' covert skills, knowledge, and affect
- Reliability of educational assessments, especially the three ways in which consistency evidence is reported for groups of test-takers (stability, alternate-form reliability, and internal consistency) and how to gauge the consistency of assessment for individual test-takers.
- The prominent role three types of validity evidence (content-related, criterion-related, and construct-related evidence) should play in building arguments to support the accuracy of test-based interpretations about students
- How to identify and eliminate assessment bias
- Construction and improvement of selected-response and constructed-response test items
- Scoring of students' responses to constructed-response tests items, especially the distinctive contribution made by well-formed rubrics
- Development and scoring of performance tests and portfolio assessments
- Designing and implementing formative-assessment procedures consonant with both research evidence and experience-based insights about the likely success of such procedures
- How to collect and interpret evidence of students' affective dispositions
- Interpreting students' performances on large-scale, standardized achievement and aptitude assessments
- Assessing English-language learners and students with disabilities
- How to appropriately and inappropriately prepare students for high-stakes tests
- How to determine the appropriateness of an accountability test for use in evaluating the quality of instruction

All but a few of these thirteen content recommendations are applicable to both classroom assessments and accountability assessments. The final recommendation regarding the evaluative appropriateness of an account-ability test, of course, refers only to accountability assessments. Similarly, the recommendation regarding how to interpret students' performances on large-scale, standardized achievement and aptitude tests is also most germane to accountability assessments rather than classroom assessments. Conversely, the recommendation that educators should learn how to devise and implement suitable formative-assessment procedures in class-rooms clearly deals with classroom assessments rather than accountability assessments. Beyond these dissimilarities, however, a professional devel-opment program aimed at promoting educators' assessment literacy should show how the bulk of the content recommended here has clear rel-evance to both classroom assessments and accountability assessments. And it doesn't need to be all that quantitative!

A lesson-learnt solution

In contrast to the five previous lesson-learnt solutions, the treatment of this sixth mistake is fairly straightforward. The problem is, simply put, that educators do not know enough about educational assessment. A factor contributing to that state of affairs is that until now, most educa-tors did not feel that they needed to know more about it.

A two-step strategy seems to be warranted in dealing with educators' lack of assessment literacy. First, both teachers and administrators must realize that they need to learn more about the fundamentals of educa-tional assessment. Second, we need to teach them about what these fun-damentals are. This two-step strategy, of course, is much easier to advocate than it is to accomplish.

Today's teachers and administrators are incredibly busy professionals. They have little spare time to tackle discretionary tasks such as learning more about educational measurement. Moreover, most of these profes-sionals, at least in their own minds, are already doing a reasonable job of what they are supposed to be doing and they've gotten by fairly well without knowing that much about measurement. So why has the situa-tion suddenly changed?

But, of course, the situation *has* changed. Test results seem to be rul-ing the roost, and many educators feel that they need to master the ba-sics of educational measurement. Clearly, when educators have accepted the idea that they need to acquire a reasonable degree of assessment acumen, then the mechanisms for them to do so must be at hand.

The second step of this strategy, therefore, is to provide professional development initiatives, preferably in many forms, so that educators can readily acquire the basic knowledge and skills they need regarding educational assessment. Above I suggested what those basics might be. Although there will surely be some difference of opinion, most members of the measurement community will agree with my content recommendations. The challenge, then, is to provide ways to transmit such information effectively and efficiently to teachers and administrators.

It goes without saying (even though I somehow seem compelled to say it) that although the thrust of this strategy revolves around the provision of assessment-related professional development programs for teachers and administrators currently working, we should make sure that preservice programs for those two groups include meaningful, obligatory treatment of assessment fundamentals. I indicated earlier that there seem to be positive signs regarding the assessment-related preparation of preservice teachers. For preservice school administrators, however, the situation is less lustrous. It is crucial for those who wish to address this problem seriously to recognize that if teachers acquire a reasonable degree of measurement knowledge but their administrative leaders do not, then the long-term dividends of teachers' assessment knowledge are apt to be squandered. If, however, we can tackle the assessment needs of in-service educators—that is, teachers *and* administrators—while addressing those same needs in pre-service educators, teachers *and* administrators, then in time this problem will surely be resolved.

Who, though, will take the lead in implementing this two-step strategy? I think there are two major groups of players who can effectively do something about enhancing educators' assessment literacy. First off, there are the officials of state education departments and school districts. Both of these entities have prominent roles to play in the education of their students. Both state and district authorities are in positions of influence to provide frequent and continuing professional development programs for their educators. Moreover, if financial resources are required—and those resources need not be gargantuan to provide many kinds of professional development programs or self-instruction materials—states and districts typically have at least some dollars to spend on those programs. A number of instructional materials designed specifically to promote assessment literacy are now beginning to be published (with blatant bias, I recommend Popham, 2006).[2]

A second group of players who can implement this two-step, lesson-learnt solution are the individuals who direct the activities of our major professional associations, such as teachers' unions, administrators' associations, and hybrid organizations such as the Association for Supervision and Curriculum Development. In most instances, such associations are eager to enhance the capabilities of their members. And in this era of test-based educational accountability, I can think of few more relevant missions than providing members with the assessment-related essentials they should have in order to function as truly competent professionals.

Clearly, a coalescence of state and district education agencies along with national and regional education associations could constitute a formidable spearhead attacking the problem of assessment illiteracy in education. Perhaps a national summit conference of all potential players, a conference potentially funded by a philanthropic foundation whose concerns extend to the nation's schools, would lead to the articulation of an effective two-step strategy for enhancing American educators' assessment literacy. It is an outcome much to be sought.

CHAPTER SEVEN

The Wyoming Story

This book is about unlearned lessons and what to do about them. In the first six chapters, I identified mistakes that I've personally seen educators make during my career. I closed out each chapter by suggesting a way to correct the mistake it addressed. In this final chapter, I'd first like to review what the six unlearned lessons were—it may help to see all six nestled together as one monster mess of mistakes. But then I want to tell you a story—a true one—about how one state's educational leaders designed and installed a statewide assessment system intended to improve instructional quality in their schools. Interestingly, by focusing on the instructional payoffs of their state's accountability tests, those educators addressed, head-on, four of the six unlearned lessons I've been yammering about in this book. I'll be telling you the Wyoming Story about what those officials did when they had to satisfy the assessment requirements of NCLB.

Oozing transparency, I want to lay out the reason I'm eager to tell about what went on in Wyoming when state educators set out to build a new kind of instructionally supportive high-stakes test. This chapter is about fixing mistakes, and what the Wyoming educators did was set up a series of accountability tests that, almost by themselves, have the ability to fix four of the six mistakes I've described. I want you to see that, at least at the state level, it is possible to learn from past errors. In Wyoming, this sort of mistake-fixing will unquestionably benefit students. Therefore I'll conclude the chapter—and the book—with a serious look at the Wyoming Story. I hope you'll find it as uplifting as I do.

THE SIX UNLEARNED LESSONS

First, though, let's look at all six of the unlearned lessons presented in the previous pages. I'll lay out each mistake, then briefly recount how I suggested that it might be corrected.

Unlearned Lesson 1: Too Many Curricular Targets. Our schools have set out an unreasonably large number of curricular aims to be taught and to be tested.

Suggested Solution Strategy. We must first fashion our curricular aims at an appropriate grain size, then prioritize them so teachers can pursue a sensible number of curricular targets.

Unlearned Lesson 2: Underutilization of Classroom Assessment. Too many teachers rely on classroom assessments only to grade or motivate students rather than as part of the formative assessment process.

Suggested Solution Strategy. Initially, we must get the word out that formative assessment is a research-proven process capable of enhancing students' learning, then we need to help teachers install this process in their own classrooms.

Unlearned Lesson 3: A Preoccupation with Instructional Process. For many educators, we see an almost obsessive preoccupation with the instructional procedures used rather than with the impact those procedures have on students.

Suggested Solution Strategy. To shift the educational community's attention from its current focus on instructional means toward curricular ends, we should turn for support to the nation's leading professional organizations, which can transmit suitable messages focused on ends and also initiate a wide variety of professional development activities that seem able to get educators to pay more attention to the consequences of teaching than to teaching itself.

Unlearned Lesson 4: The Absence of Affective Assessment. At the moment, there is essentially a complete absence of assessment devices suitable for measuring the attitudes, interests, and values of student groups.

Suggested Solution Strategy. We should provide teachers with a wide range of optional-use affective inventories along with professional development addressing how to defensibly promote appropriate student affect.

Unlearned Lesson 5: Instructionally Insensitive Accountability Tests. Almost all of the tests being used to evaluate the quality of our nation's schools are incapable of doing so.

Suggested Solution Strategy. We must replace instructionally insensitive accountability tests with those that are able to distinguish between effectively and ineffectively taught students.

Unlearned Lesson 6: Abysmal Assessment Literacy. At a time when test-based accountability dramatically influences what goes on in our schools, far too few educators understand the fundamentals of educational measurement.

Suggested Solution Strategy. We first need to help educators recognize how imperative it is for them to become assessment literate and identify the areas in which they need to deepen their knowledge. Then we must provide diverse avenues for them to acquire assessment literacy.

These, then, are the six unlearned lessons I've seen up close over the years. As noted, some of these mistakes represent errors of commission and some errors of omission. But regardless of how any of these errors is classified, it most definitely ends up lowering the quality of education we provide our students.

I want to turn to the accomplishments of a group of state employees who decided to directly address some of the problems in their schools caused by traditionally conceived accountability tests. As I finished writing this book, the federal law most influencing U.S. schools was NCLB (the most recent reauthorization of ESEA of 1965), which gives considerable latitude to how states comply with its requirements. When ESEA is again reauthorized, probably in a year or two, there may be more, or perhaps fewer, options for state officials. For instance, a revised federal statute might rely more heavily on district-level accountability or, in contrast, could require a shift toward a national, federally administered accountability program. But, at the moment, the people who occupy leadership positions in state education departments have considerable influence on how a state satisfies the demands of NCLB. Let's see how, in one state, educators did just that.

ONE STATE'S EFFORTS

As indicated above, when NCLB—the current incarnation of a nearly 40-year-old federal statute—was signed into law by President Bush on January 8, 2002, it sent a serious shudder through educators in all fifty states. Not only did the law call for more than twice as much testing of each state's students, but for schools and districts that failed to improve their students' scores sufficiently on those tests, serious penalties were in store. Any state education official who, in 2002, devoted even modest attention to the provisions of NCLB realized that, unlike many of its predecessors, this new version of ESEA packed punch aplenty.

Building a different kind of accountability test

Administrators in the Wyoming Department of Education (WDE) were definitely aware in 2002 that the stakes associated with NCLB's tests were substantially higher than in the preceding version of ESEA, that is, the 1994 Improving America's Schools Act (IASA). In NCLB, for instance, if schools and districts were not able to get enough of their students classified proficient (or better), then many citizens would surely regard those low-performing schools and districts as "failing."[1] Moreover, failing schools would soon be on the receiving end of some serious sanctions that, in time, could lead to their complete disappearance. WDE leaders saw clearly that any tests capable of having such a great impact on their state's schools would certainly exert considerable influence on what went on in Wyoming classrooms. The state's teachers would, understandably, try to get their schools and districts to succeed on these newly imposed NCLB tests by carrying out their instruction so success seemed more likely. The 2002 version of ESEA would have a profound impact on the way Wyoming teachers taught.

So, while most states satisfied NCLB's demand for new tests at more grade levels by using the same kinds of accountability tests they had been using until then, WDE officials made a decisively different choice.

Annette Bohling, an attorney and former classroom teacher, was at that time the deputy superintendent of schools for Wyoming, and she persuaded her WDE colleagues that this was a remarkable educational opportunity for their state. Thus, even though WDE had only recently installed a set of new, albeit fairly traditional, statewide tests to satisfy the provisions of IASA, Bohling and her colleagues decided to create a series of new accountability tests for NCLB that were patently intended to support improved instruction in Wyoming. They then set about developing a request for proposals (RFP) to invite commercial test vendors to build the new test series, which ultimately became known as the Proficiency Assessments for Wyoming Students (PAWS).

The RFP issued by WDE called for the creation of NCLB accountability tests that were unequivocally *intended to improve instruction* in Wyoming's classrooms. Three features that Bohling and her coworkers called for in the new tests (for grades 3-8 and one grade in high school) were especially important. WDE wanted accountability tests for NCLB based on:

1. A limited number of assessment targets to be measured by the tests
2. Clear descriptions of each cognitive skill (or body of knowledge) measured
3. A sufficient number of test items measuring each assessment target

During the time the RFP was being circulated, WDE curriculum specialists attempted to reduce the number of curricular aims to be assessed on the new tests. Wyoming's previous accountability tests had attempted, rather unsuccessfully, to assess students' mastery of the entire array of curricular aims that had been approved for Wyoming's public schools. What Bohling and her staff set out to do was *prioritize* those too-numerous content standards so that the most significant cognitive skills embodied in those standards would be assessed by the soon-to-be-built NCLB tests. Although Wyoming teachers would definitely be able to promote students' mastery of less significant state content standards, the most educationally significant of those standards would be identified in the form of high-level cognitive skills. Wyoming students' mastery of those demanding cognitive skills would be what was assessed by the state's new NCLB tests.

WDE staffers sought the counsel of experienced teachers and administrators throughout the state to help them identify the cognitive skills to be measured by the new NCLB tests. The quest was for a modest number of unarguably significant cognitive skills that would function as both the targets to be measured by the new NCLB assessments and the high-priority instructional targets for Wyoming schools. Ultimately, twenty-two challenging cognitive skills were identified for the new NCLB tests, eight in reading, two in writing, and twelve in mathematics. These skills were formulated so that, if taught effectively, they could definitely be achieved by Wyoming students.

Next, for each of these twenty-two skills, an assessment description was generated by WDE staff. Each of these assessment descriptions provided a relatively brief depiction of the essential attributes of a particular PAWS skill. Written in teacher-palatable language, these assessment descriptions were intended to give Wyoming teachers a clear idea about the nature of the skill to be assessed so that those teachers could aim instruction at students' generalized mastery of the skill itself, rather than merely getting students to answer a particular set of questions.

Finally, because there were relatively few skills to be assessed, it was possible to include enough items on any PAWS test so that teachers could make a reasonably accurate estimate of each student's mastery of each skill. After a group of Wyoming teachers and curriculum experts had reviewed the assessment descriptions, they indicated how many test items must be on the test to accurately measure each PAWS skill. (Certain kinds of PAWS test items are weighted more heavily than others.)

Clearly, what Bohling and her colleagues were trying to do was design accountability tests so those tests would have a positive *instructional* impact on what took place in Wyoming. It's perhaps surprising to learn that such an instructionally oriented approach to state-level accountability testing is rare. Bohling had foreseen that NCLB, because of its potential penalties, would have a whopping impact on how Wyoming's teachers functioned. She wanted to make sure that this impact would benefit students.

Geographically, Wyoming is a large state, but it has a smaller enrollment than many of its counterparts. Given the modest number of students, the staff of the state's education department (that is, WDE employees) is relatively small. Moreover, when Bohling initiated her ambitious plan to build instructionally beneficial accountability tests to satisfy NCLB, the number of people on the WDE assessment staff was not only tiny but also relatively inexperienced at building the kind of large-scale tests required by NCLB. Under Bohling's leadership, that small assessment staff learned lots, and learned it fast! There was no other choice. The three pivotal players in WDE's creation of PAWS were Lesley Wangberg (director of assessment), Bill Herrera (assistant director of assessment), and Charlene Turner (director of alternate assessment). These three, all of them former teachers, were able to bring a classroom-engendered instructional perspective to the building of PAWS. In retrospect, their lack of familiarity with "assessment as usual" probably was a blessing in that PAWS was supposed to be a test that not only supplied accurate evaluative information about schools, but also served as a catalyst for better classroom instruction—clearly *not* assessment as usual.

What insights can we pick up from these opening acts of Wyoming's PAWS experience? Well, for one thing, there's a need for a forward-looking leader who wants state tests to stimulate improved instruction so students will be better educated. In Wyoming, Annette Bohling was that person. Second, that leader must have sufficient clout to move assessment personnel in the appropriate direction. Again, as deputy state superintendent, Bohling was that person. And, finally, a talented support staff is needed, whether or not they are steeped in traditional ways of thinking about educational tests. The support staff must make sure that the external assessment firm hired to create and administer the state's tests will do what it is directed to do. In Wangberg, Herrera, and Turner, WDE had the necessary core of an extraordinarily competent staff.

Could other states do something similar with their own accountability tests? You bet they could! But without a perceptive leader who has ample clout and is bent on creating instructionally influential accountability tests, and without the support of a capable staff, the likelihood of installing a "PAWS-like" set of assessments is minimal.

Selection of a test contractor

When the WDE assessment team issued their RFP to the nation's testing companies, they tried to frame it so it would be apparent to bidders that Wyoming was not looking for a "same-old, same-old" sort of accountability test. Statements in the RFP attested to the need for an accountability test that would have a positive impact on the state's schools. Indeed, it may have been this call for "a new, instructionally relevant" sort of NCLB test that enticed nine assessment companies to bid on the project. In view of Wyoming's relatively small enrollments, this was a surprisingly large show of interest in building the PAWS tests.

After a large of committee of Wyoming educators and assessment specialists reviewed all nine proposals, Harcourt Assessment of San Antonio, Texas, was chosen to build the PAWS tests, administer them, and report results to the appropriate constituencies. The relatively small WDE assessment team obviously hoped that the selected contractor would become an active partner in optimizing the instructional impact of the PAWS tests. It soon became apparent, however, that although Harcourt personnel were remarkably skilled in carrying out the many traditional operations called for as part of statewide testing, they had little to contribute on the instructional side of the equation. Putting it plainly, Harcourt staff were well-versed in traditional psychometric procedures but had little to offer when it came to making PAWS an assessment system that boosted instructional quality.

Under NCLB, it is expected that each state will appoint a technical advisory committee (TAC) that periodically advises assessment personnel about the merits of their state's accountability tests. Typically, these TACs are composed of traditional measurement specialists who tend to regard statewide tests, not surprisingly, in a fairly traditional manner. When WDE appointed its TAC for PAWS, however, most members of the six-person group were chiefly known for their instructional expertise rather than their conversance with conventional large-scale testing programs. The Wyoming TAC met often during the early months of PAWS's construction, often urging the contractor (Harcourt) to play a stronger contributory role in regard to the test's instructional dividends. Harcourt personnel, however, were rarely able to respond to these entreaties. It became apparent to TAC members, and to the WDE assessment team, that Harcourt was decisively limited in what it could supply in the way of assessment-relevant instructional insights.

The WDE assessment team's experience in trying to make the PAWS tests instructionally helpful made it clear that when the time came to either renew the contract with Harcourt or to seek a new contractor, care would need to be taken in spelling out unequivocally any instructionally relevant operations it was expected the contractor to perform. Thus, in the fall of 2008, a new RFP was issued to administer and score PAWS. Four bidders responded, and at this writing no contractor has yet to be chosen.

But what was seen in the selection of the first PAWS contractor is worth noting. It is unwise to assume that a testing firm is bristling with instructional acumen, ready to trade pedagogical insights with state assessment personnel. Indeed, quite the opposite is apt to be true. Thus, it is imperative to spell out in any RFP (and to solidify later in a formal contract) precisely what, if anything, a test contractor is supposed to do on the instructional side of the ledger. In most instances, instructional insights are not apt to spring serendipitously from today's testing contractors.

Setting passing standards

As soon as the PAWS tests were about ready to be administered, the assessment team had to establish cut scores on all tests for all grade levels so that once the scores were available, students could be classified as below basic, basic, proficient, or advanced. NCLB calls for an ever-increasing proportion of students to be classified as proficient or advanced, all the way up to 2014, when this remarkably ambitious federal law requires all students to score at a proficient or advanced level. And, because schools or districts with an insufficient number of students moving toward the 2014 target will be identified as having failed to make adequate yearly progress (AYP), it was obviously important to set PAWS cut scores with consummate care.

Because WDE staff realized that a mistake at this important point in the development of a PAWS program could be disastrous (at the very least from a public relations perspective), a decision was made to ask a prestigious blue-ribbon panel to recommend cut scores to the state superintendent of schools, Dr. Jim McBride. Accordingly, at a two-day meeting in Jackson Hole, a high-visibility panel of prominent Wyoming citizens considered (1) students' past scores on Wyoming's existing accountability tests, (2) students' scores on trial versions of the PAWS items, and (3) students' scores on the National Assessment of Educational Progress. The blue-ribbon panel also reviewed recommendations from several groups of Wyoming educators specifically asked for advice

SIDEBAR 7.1

Assessment Companies: Submarine Builders

Suppose you wanted to buy a submarine. Yes, I know full well that few of us ever really need to buy a submarine. But, just to humor me for a moment, imagine that you want to acquire your very own submarine. If you prefer, it can even be yellow.

Well, if you were on a mission to snare your personal underwater craft, I would urge you not to go to an aircraft-carrier store. It's true that aircraft carriers and submarines have some things in common—but not enough. Aircraft carriers are found on top of what submarines are found under. It's a nontrivial difference.

There are parallels to this potential ocean vessel mix-up; for example, when policymakers suggest that we turn to the nation's testing companies for educational solutions—that is, to the dozen or so major firms that build, administer, and score educational tests. Given our almost pathological preoccupation with students' test performance these days, some policymakers assume that if testing companies would only turn their minds to it, they could lead us out of our current dilemma where test scores seem to trump every other sort of evaluative evidence.

In recent years, many large testing companies have come out with new products they are billing as diagnostic assessments. These new assessment tools are being marketed with a claim that teachers who use them can get a solid fix on an individual student's strengths and weaknesses. In many instances, however, these diagnostic poseurs are little more than a flock of test items, each of which is supposed to be aligned with a typically ill-defined curricular standard. Because these "instructionally useful" assessments are destined to be sold in a nation whose curricular preferences vary, the test-makers dare not spell out too specifically what their tests assess, for such specificity would make the assessments less appealing to many would-be purchasers. To make diagnostic sense out of such silliness, however, a teacher must wade through an overwhelming number of test results to figure out what some kids know and some kids don't. Diagnosing need not be drudgery, yet some testing companies are definitely peddling diagnostic tests that busy teachers can't intuitively interpret.

What we need to recognize about assessment companies is that they do a marvelous job of what they have always done. Oh, sure, with so many millions of tests to score, sometimes scoring or reporting mistakes are made. But, on the whole, testing outfits do a solid job of building and scoring the kinds of tests they have always built and scored. But those tests are dominantly intended to provide comparative interpretations of test-takers' performances. For almost a century in this country, the established giants of the educational testing industry have built tests allowing us to compare examinees' scores. We can determine that Wally scored at the 87th percentile while Wilma scored at the 76th, relative to the performance of a norm group of previous test-takers. This sort of test has always been needed by the world, and probably always will be.

Tests that do a good job of detecting relative differences among test-takers are especially useful whenever there is a fixed quota with more applicants than openings. Indeed, whenever an important decision hangs on identifying which test-takers are "best" or "worst," then comparative tests do a terrific job. And testing companies know how to do all the technical stuff needed to make those tests work well. They can churn out different test forms measuring the same thing and make needed statistical adjustments if it turns out that some test forms differ in difficulty. They can even detect cheating on tests by spotting atypical erasure patterns on students' answer sheets. Yes, the nation's large assessment companies are darn good at what they do.

But when it comes to tests that are intended to help educators do a better instructional job, most testing companies don't have a clue. And why should they? Tests intended to differentiate among test-takers need not make a contribution to instruction. Just think about it; if a comparison-oriented test did a great job of helping teachers instruct their students—so great that almost all students were knocking the top off the test—then there would be no meaningful variation among those high-scoring students and, as a consequence, comparative interpretations would be impossible.

I concede that a few of the nation's testing companies are gingerly approaching matters more related to instruction and several are beginning to offer professional development sessions for educators. Moreover, some of those sessions deal with instructional issues. However, for the most part, you must understand that testing companies know squat about instruction.

When people are really good at something, it is tough to criticize them for not being good at something else. Such is the situation with respect to the testing industry. America's testing companies are loaded with skilled psychometricians who know their onions. And, through the years, these testing companies have assembled strong staffs simply swimming in psychometric suave. Testing firms really have had no need to nurture any sort of in-house instructional capacity. There was no need for folks with instructional moxie.

continued

SIDEBAR 7.1 *continued*

So, unless some of these testing firms consciously set out to give something more than token attention to instruction, I urge you not to look to them
for solutions to our nation's *educational* problems. Today's testing outfits simply don't have the staff to tackle the sorts of education-related problems I've
been addressing in this book.

What we really need now is an educationally relevant submarine, and
today's testing companies only know how to build aircraft carriers.

---

regarding PAWS cut scores. That panel included Wyoming's governor,
the president of the University of Wyoming, several prominent state legislators, and a number of prominent leaders from the state. (After two
days of intensive discussion of the data, the panel recommended cut
scores to Superintendent McBride, which he accepted with only minor
adjustments.

Two points are worth making regarding setting PAWS cut scores. First,
because of the importance of this activity, WDE personnel assembled an
influential and impressive group of individuals to offer recommendations
to Dr. McBride. Second, because of their active involvement in this enterprise, all members of the blue-ribbon panel became conversant with the
atypical nature of their state's new NCLB accountability tests.

Had you been a panelist during that two-day conclave in Jackson
Hole, you surely would have left the session with a far better understanding of what the PAWS tests were supposed to accomplish. Moreover, the panelists would have recognized that PAWS was not intended
to be a traditional educational achievement test. Thus the standard-set-
ting process was a double mission—the generation of clearly defensible
cut scores, and an effort to educate influential Wyoming policymakers.

Making PAWS influence instruction

Remember, the rationale for PAWS from the very get-go was that it
would be an accountability testing program capable of both providing
evaluative evidence of school performance and spurring instructional
improvements. Let's see how that segment of the story turned out.

Well, for starters, the decision to use a sufficient number of test items to measure each of the twenty-two PAWS skills made it possible to provide legitimate diagnostic information to the state's teachers. Distributors of many current educational tests claim that their tests supply diagnostic evidence to teachers but, upon closer inspection, those tests are heavier on claim than on diagnosis. But this was not so with PAWS. One of the instructional diagnosis systems devised by the WDE assessment team is known as the *traffic-signal process*. Here's how it works.

The PAWS tests are administered each spring. Within a couple of weeks after students have completed those tests, panels of seasoned Wyoming classroom teachers meet to provide recommendations for their colleagues as to whether students need additional instruction regarding each of the PAWS skills. Panels of eight to twelve educators meet at each grade level and in each subject to give all Wyoming teachers a "green light," "yellow light," or "red light" for each student on every PAWS skill. The panelists have access to the actual items administered only a few days earlier, and they also see how Wyoming students performed on those items.

Based on sometimes intense discussions, the teacher panels identify the number of items a student would need to have answered correctly in order to be given a green light. A green light on a particular PAWS skill indicates that the student apparently does not need additional instruction on this skill. For example, on a reading skill measured by nine items, the panel of teachers might decide that a student who answered eight or nine items correctly probably doesn't need additional instruction. Students scoring at that level would get a green light. The panel might decide that students who answered five or fewer items correctly should be given a red light, indicating that they almost certainly needed more instruction on that skill. So, if a student answered six or seven items correctly, it would be yellow light time, indicating that the student may or may not need additional instruction on this particular skill. In this case, the classroom teacher should use additional evidence, if possible, to reach a decision regarding additional instruction.

These "traffic signals" are given to teachers when they get their students' results on PAWS prior to the end of the school year. The teachers can see how every student performed on each PAWS skill, and there are enough items per skill to give the teacher a reasonably accurate diagnostic estimate for each student. Teachers can also look at the traffic signals for their entire class and note which PAWS skills have loads of yellow or red signals. It would seem that those skills are not among a teacher's most effective instructional efforts, calling perhaps for different instructional activities in the next school year.

Incidentally, the PAWS traffic signal process was installed only after WDE staff had carried out a small-scale experiment in which two teacher panels were randomly constituted, then independently arrived at appropriate cut scores for each skill's traffic signal report. When the separate judgments of the two teacher-panels were compared, they were remarkably similar.

In addition to getting these traffic signal reports for each student instructed during the previous school year, all teachers also get a report early in the following year for their incoming students. These green-yellow-red designations are particularly helpful for instructional planning because the twenty-two PAWS skills remain the same throughout the grades. A math skill might be more complex in the higher grades, of course, but when teachers get an accurate idea of which students need more work in particular skills, they can appropriately tailor their instruction.

But the traffic-signal process gets even better. After the panels finish setting their cut scores for each PAWS skill—and remember, these are seasoned Wyoming teachers who know what students at certain grade levels are typically capable of—these teachers consider each skill in relation to the performance of that year's students on the PAWS items. They then offer instructional suggestions to their colleagues throughout the state. These suggestions, based on actual student performance on actual PAWS items, describe instructional ideas for each PAWS skill, especially for students who seem to be having trouble with a particular skill.

Teachers in Wyoming do not have to pay attention to the traffic-signal reports, or to the teacher panel's instructional suggestions. The teacher panels are simply groups of experienced teachers offering suggestions to their colleagues about how to do a better job. But if I were a teacher whose students had performed poorly on a given PAWS skill last year, and in my class this year I found scads of students with yellow-light and red-light reports for that same skill, I'd take the suggestions of my colleagues very seriously. The traffic-signal process is an example of an instructional dividend flowing naturally from an accountability testing program that's been deliberately fashioned to provide an instructional payoff.

The WDE staff also took action to ensure that the PAWS tests accurately reflected the quality of instruction provided to students on the actual items being produced by Harcourt, the test contractor. WDE insisted that, in addition to the scrutiny given to all items under development on an accountability test, those items must be evaluated on the basis of their instructional sensitivity. In a conventional review of items destined for a high-stakes accountability test, each potential item is typically judged by a panel of reviewers who evaluate whether an item is properly aligned with the skill or content standard it is supposed to be measuring. Each item is also reviewed for assessment bias; that is, an item is evaluated to see whether it might offend or unfairly penalize test-takers because of personal characteristics, such as race, gender, ethnicity, and so on. All would-be PAWS items were reviewed on the basis of both curricular alignment and assessment bias.

However, all PAWS items also are judged according to the likelihood that they will help accurately determine the quality of instruction provided for the particular skill being measured. Item reviewers are therefore asked, "If a teacher has given students reasonably effective instruction on the PAWS skill being measured by this item, is it likely that a substantial majority of that teacher's students will answer the item correctly?" As you can see, this item-review question is intended to increase the probability that the PAWS tests will be instructionally sensitive. Clearly, if the PAWS tests cannot accurately distinguish between effective and ineffective instruction, then the long-term dividends of PAWS on instruction in the state will be diminished. That's because both effective instruction and ineffective instruction are apt to be misidentified.

Best-laid plans

Two other instructionally oriented hopes of the WDE assessment team perished during the early years of PAWS. Because this was billed as a true story, let's see what went awry.

Okay, back to the main theme of the Wyoming story, namely, the quest for a set of NCLB tests that would stimulate ever-improving classroom instruction. Because the WDE assessment team, not too long out of the classroom, recognized the importance of urging teachers to get the most out of the PAWS assessment program, WDE assessment personnel became thoroughly conversant with the essentials of classroom formative assessment. For more than a decade, solid research has indicated that when teachers use evidence from classroom assessments to adjust their instructional activities, or students use it to adjust their learning tactics, sizeable improvements in student learning takes place (see chapter 2.) Put simply, the formative assessment process works, and it works big time.

So, soon after the first round of PAWS tests were up and running, WDE staff worked out plans to develop—in-house—illustrative assessment tools that teachers could use when they employed the formative assessment process to promote their students' mastery of the twenty-two skills. Moreover, because the identification of the learning progressions underlying these skills is so very crucial to formative assessment, WDE staff decided to create an illustrative array of these progressions for various PAWS skills at several grade levels. A learning progression, incidentally, is the set of building blocks—that is, the cognitive subskills or bodies of enabling knowledge—students must master en route to mastering a more remote curricular aim (in this instance, one of the PAWS skills).

The WDE assessment team's plan was to create a collection of suitable classroom testing procedures—both formal and informal—that might be employed as part of the formative-assessment process, and several exemplary learning progressions. Once these illustrative materials were in hand, WDE staff intended to provide intensive professional development for the state's teachers and administrators, making clear that by focusing on the consequences of instruction, as indicated by students' performance on the PAWS skills and the building blocks leading up to them, teachers could capitalize on the instructionally oriented state tests that had been created for them. It was a wonderful plan, made possible chiefly by the presence of an instructionally supportive assessment program. But what had been planned never took place.

Plans on paper and the implementation of those plans in the real world often differ. At precisely the time the WDE staff had their PAWS tests up and running, and immediately before Wyoming educators began to benefit from PAWS instructional features, the U.S. Department of Education (USDE) installed a peer-review process. This process changed everything in Wyoming, putting an end to the state's plans to get instructional mileage out of PAWS. Let's see why.

The peer-review process is a form of guidance in which federally appointed individuals who are knowledgeable about assessment review the adequacy of what a state is doing in its assessment program to comply with the provisions of NCLB. Theoretically, this approach to the scrutiny of state assessment plans and procedures makes a sack of sense to me. That's because it can be used to identify state assessment endeavors in which measurement mistakes might lead to educational decisions that are harmful to students.

In the case of the Wyoming PAWS, however, there was a state's unabashed attempt to do something decidedly different, namely, to build a set of accountability assessments to strengthen instruction in the state. The PAWS tests were, by design, not traditional state-level assessments But, frankly, the PAWS tests were evaluated by traditional peers who brought traditional perspectives to the peer review of an untraditional assessment program.

As a consequence of peer reviewers who looked at PAWS though traditional psychometric lenses, the program was turned down several times by the USDE process. If a state program is turned down too often by peer reviewers, there is not only the prospect of public embarrassment, but substantial federal dollars are also certain to be withheld. Neither of those consequences is apt to be viewed with elation by officials in any state education department.

And so it was that for almost two years, the WDE assessment staff was obliged to spend an enormous amount of time trying to obtain peer-review approval of the PAWS program. Members of the Wyoming TAC looked on with dismay at the lack of attention being given to PAWS-related instructional initiatives. Yet it was obvious that the WDE assessment team had no time to deal with those aspects of the PAWS program, and no time to work with teachers on how to use an instructionally illuminating testing program. There was no time because the WDE assessment team was required to leap through traditional hoops that, in many instances, were fundamentally inconsistent with an atypical, instructionally oriented state assessment program.

I have no quarrel with setting up and implementing a peer-review process. It is prudent to have colleagues judge each others' work because our ultimate concern is what will be good for children educationally. What happened in Wyoming, however, was an unwarranted triumph of traditional psychometric thinking over an innovative effort to help kids learn better. As noted earlier, the WDE assessment team is relatively small. Its members are talented, although they happen to reside in the Mountain Time Zone, they still have only twenty-four hours a day available to them. The WDE staff was quite literally crippled for about two years by a straight-jacketing federal review process. It is my hope that now, with peer-review approval formally in hand, WDE assessment personnel can get back to what they wanted to do in the first place—educate Wyoming students more effectively.

Whether or not you approve of NCLB, it is difficult to dismiss the worthiness of that federal statute's overriding educational goal, namely, to get many more American children to attain proficient levels of achievement. The centerpiece of NCLB's accountability strategy, of course, was using students' accountability test scores to trigger instructional improvements. Yet, when Wyoming deliberately tried to build instruction-enhancing accountability tests in an effort to make NCLB work most effectively, they were whacked by a peer-review process conceived in a totally conventional psychometric fashion. In a very real sense, federal officials had installed a staid, safe review process that penalized states for trying to make the instructional thrust of a federal law work properly. In whatever form a newly reauthorized ESEA finally arrives, if the peer-review process is continued, we must make certain that it nurtures, rather than negates, the efforts of educators who want their tests to benefit education.

A Wyoming reprise

Looking back, what we see in Wyoming is an instructionally oriented assessment initiative that turns out to address four of the six unlearned lessons treated in this book. First, state education leaders have prioritized Wyoming's numerous content standards by deriving from those standards a manageable number of cognitive skills, and those twenty-two skills serve as the curricular focus for the state's new accountability tests. Second, all potential PAWS items are reviewed on the basis of their instructional sensitivity, thereby making it more likely the PAWS tests will provide accurate information on the quality of instruction provided in Wyoming schools and districts. Finally, by planning to provide support for formative assessment, which in turn entails paying great attention to the outcome of instruction, the state intends to remedy two of the other mistakes treated in this book, the preoccupation with instructional process and the underutilization of classroom assessment.

I hope that some time in the future, WDE assessment personnel will consider adding affective assessment to their statewide assessment program, or at least teach Wyoming's teachers how to create their own affective inventories. And, of course, I hope the WDE assessment team will find time to promote greater assessment literacy among Wyoming educators. But setting my yearnings aside, let's be realistic—four out of six is surely passing!

Check-out time

I'm not sure what the future holds for accountability assessment in Wyoming. Perhaps PAWS will flourish and the state's students will benefit as much from those tests as had been originally hoped. On the other hand, as we saw in the case of a hamstringing federal review process, even competent and well-intentioned professionals can be deflected.

What happened in Wyoming took place at the state level, of course. But what I wanted to convey was how, in Wyoming, one person's efforts led to far-reaching changes in the way a state's children are being assessed and, as a consequence, being educated. One person.

Not all readers have access to the corridors of power. Some, of course, may have influence at the state or even national level, while others are busy trying to improve their districts, schools, or classrooms, whether as parents, teachers, or administrators. Each of us has a range of options for taking action on these unlearned lessons: sharing our concerns with colleagues, enlisting the support of professional associations, reaching out to foundations, or swaying public opinion through blogs, letters to the editor, or other advocacy strategies targeting the media. Those of you who are teacher educators may strive to reach students one by one.

The older I get, the more pleased I am to have stumbled into a career as an educator. As a youth, I never yearned to be a teacher—not even once. Indeed, not until I was a senior in college and began exploring what I might do to earn a salary after graduation did I really think seriously about becoming a teacher. At that time in my life I regarded really small children as rather repellant. Had I been obliged to teach those little squirmers, I surely would have chosen another field. Thankfully I found teenagers tolerable, so becoming a high school teacher seemed a possibility. As I take stock of what I've been up to as a teacher over the years, I realize how important it is to take part in educating the young members of our species. Being a teacher is monstrously more important than I thought it was when I initially decided to become one.

Well, through the years, I've seen many instances in which I thought an unwise educational policy was messing up the children. And, more than a few times, I set out to try to change one of those policies. In my many attempts to change unsound educational policies, I have experienced failure up close and personal, in a wide variety of ways. Most of the time my change efforts could be generously characterized as altogether ineffectual. Were I to recount all of my great aspirations and unsuccessful initiatives, we'd end up with another book longer than this one.

Here I am, however, in this book's final chapter, urging you to try to alter one or more educational policies that are having an adverse impact on kids. You might, understandably, regard my urging as mildly hypocritical. After all, the vast majority of my own policy-changing initiatives have flopped. Moreover, if you try to fix any of the six problems I've treated in this book, odds are that you are apt to fail as well. But then you might not.

And even if, despite your best efforts, you do fail to modify an ill-conceived educational policy, you will still have tried to bring about changes that would have benefited children. Given a choice between tried-but-failed and never-tried-at-all, I'd rather take the former option every time.

When you are getting ready to wheel your shopping cart up for that final check-out (the one in the sky) and you look back at your own career, if you can say in good conscience that you tried to change policies that were harmful to children—even if your efforts were unsuccessful— well, that's not a terrible way to check out.

Notes

Chapter 1

1. WestEd, *Responses to Critical Questions.*
2. Rabinowitz, "Oregon Content Standards and Assessment System Evaluation."
3. Marzano and Haystead, *Making Standards Work in the Classroom,* 7.
4. Roach, *Strategies for Revising Content Standards to Ensure Effectiveness in Guiding Assessment and Instruction.*

Chapter 2

1. Popham, 2008b.
2. Black and Wiliam, "Assessment and Classroom Learning."
3. Natriello, "The Impact of Evaluation Process on Students"; Crooks, "The Impact of Classroom Evaluation Practices on Students."
4. Black and Wiliam, "Assessment and Classroom Learning," 61.
5. Black and Wiliam, "Inside the Black Box."
6. Black and Wiliam, "Assessment and Classroom Learning," 61.
7. Black and Wiliam, "Assessment and Classroom Learning," 17.
8. Black and Wiliam, "Assessment and Classroom Learning."
9. Wylie, "Tight but Loose."

Chapter 3

1. Kohn, "It's Not What We Teach."
2. Kohn, "It's Not What We Teach," 26.

Sidebar 3.1

1. Cantor, *The Dynamics of Learning.*

Sidebar 3.3

1. ASCD, 1988
2. ASCD, 1988, 56–77.

Chapter 4

1. Bloom, Engelhart, Furst, Hill, and Krathwohl, *Taxonomy of Educational Objectives.*
2. Krathwohl, Bloom, and Masia, *Taxonomy of Educational Objectives: Handbook II.*
3. Anderson and Bourke, *Assessing Affective Characteristics in the Schools*; Popham, 2008a.

Chapter 5

1. Flesch, *Why Johnny Can't Read.*
2. Gardner, *Multiple Intelligences.*
3. Popham, *The Truth about Testing,* 65, 73.

Chapter 6

1. Stiggins, "Assessment *for* Learning"; Popham (2008a and 2008b).
2. Popham, *Mastering Assessment.*

Chapter 7

1. Popham, 2005

Bibliography

Anderson, Lorin W., and Sid F. Bourke. *Assessing Affective Characteristics in the Schools* (2nd ed.). Mahwah, NJ: Lawrence Erlbaum, 2000.

Black, Paul, and Dylan Wiliam. "Assessment and Classroom Learning." *Assessment in Education: Principles, Policy and Practice* 5, no. 1 (1998a): 7–68.

Black, Paul, and Dylan Wiliam. "Inside the Black Box: Raising Standards through Classroom Assessment." *Phi Delta Kappan* 80, no. 2 (1998b, October): 139–148.

Bloom, B. S., M. D. Engelhart, E. J. Furst, W. H. Hill, and D. R. Krathwohl. *Taxonomy of Educational Objectives: Handbook I: The Cognitive Domain.* New York: David McKay, 1956.

Cantor, Nathaniel. *The Dynamics of Learning.* Buffalo, NY: Foster and Stewart, 1946.

Crooks, Terry. "The Impact of Classroom Evaluation Practices on Students." *Review of Educational Research* 58, no. 4 (1988): 438–481.

Flesch, Rudolph. *Why Johnny Can't Read: And What You Can Do About It.* New York: Harper, 1955.

Gardner, Howard. *Multiple Intelligences: The Theory in Practice.* New York: Basic, 1993.

Kohn, Alfie. "It's Not What We Teach, It's What They Learn." *Education Week,* September 10, 2008, p. 32.

Krathwohl, David R., Benjamin. S. Bloom, and Bertram. B. Masia. *Taxonomy of Educational Objectives: Handbook II: Affective Domain.* New York: David McKay, 1964.

Mager, Robert F. *Preparing Objectives for Programmed Instruction.* San Francisco: Fearon Press, 1962.

Marzano, Robert J., and Mark W. Haystead. *Making Standards Work in the Classroom.* Alexandria, VA: Association for Supervision and Curriculum Development, 2008.

Natriello, Gary. "The Impact of Evaluation Process on Students." *Educational Psychologist* 22, no. 2 (1987): 155–175.

Popham, W. James. "Judgment-Based Teacher Evaluation." In *Teacher Evaluation: Six Prescriptions for Success,* edited by Sarah J. Stanley and W.J. Popham, 56–77. Alexandria, VA: Association for Supervision and Curriculum Development, 1988.

Popham, W. James. *The Truth about Testing: An Educator's Call to Action.* Alexandria, VA: Association for Supervision and Curriculum Development, 2001.

Popham, W. James. *America's "Failing" Schools: How Parents and Teachers Can Cope with No Child Left Behind.* New York: Routledge, 2005.

Popham, W. James. *Mastering Assessment: A Self-Service System For Educators.* New York: Routledge, 2006.

Popham, W. James. *Classroom Assessment: What Teachers Need to Know* (5th ed.). Boston: Allyn and Bacon, 2008a.

Popham, W. James. *Transformative Assessment.* Alexandria, VA: Association for Supervision and Curriculum Development, 2008b.

Rabinowitz, Stanley. "Oregon Content Standards and Assessment System Evaluation: Critical Questions Report." Paper presented at annual assessment conference, Oregon Department of Education, Portland, Oregon, August 8, 2007.

Roach, Michael. *Strategies for Revising Content Standards to Ensure Effectiveness in Guiding Assessment and Instruction.* Presentation at the National Student Assessment Conference, Council of Chief State School Officers, Orlando, Florida, June 15–18, 2008.

Stiggins, Rick. "Assessment *for* Learning: A Key to Motivation and Achievement." *Edge, 2.* Bloomington, Indiana: Phi Delta Kappa, November/December 2006.

WestEd. *Responses to Critical Questions: Oregon Standards and Assessments Evaluation Report, August 31.* San Francisco: Author, 2007.

Wylie, E. Caroline. "Tight but Loose: Scaling Up Teacher Professional Development in Diverse Contexts" (Educational Testing Service Research Report, RR-08-29). Princeton, NJ: Educational Testing Service, June 2008.

Acknowledgment

I wish to acknowledge the contributions to this book of Caroline Chauncey and her colleagues at Harvard Education Press. It was Caroline's initial suggestion that I write such a book and, during the more than two years it took me to get underway, it was her polite but persistent prodding that prevented me from forgetting the idea. Finally, when the manuscript actually arrived in Cambridge, it was she who supplied much needed editorial guidance at precisely the right moment. Regarding this project, whether indicted or not, Caroline is clearly a coconspirator. I thank her.

About the Author

W. James Popham has spent the bulk of his educational career as a teacher. His first teaching assignment was in a small high school in eastern Oregon, where he taught English and social studies while serving as yearbook advisor, class sponsor, and unpaid tennis coach. That recompense meshed ideally with the quality of his coaching.

Most of Dr. Popham's teaching career took place at UCLA, where, for nearly thirty years, he taught courses in instructional methods for prospective teachers and courses in evaluation and measurement for graduate students. At UCLA he won several distinguished teaching awards and, in January 2000, he was recognized by *UCLA Today* as one of UCLA's top twenty professors of the twentieth century. (He notes that the twentieth century was a full-length century, unlike the current abbreviated one.) In 1992, Dr. Popham took early retirement from UCLA upon learning that emeritus professors received free parking.

Because at UCLA he was acutely aware of the perishability of professors who failed to publish, Dr. Popham spent his nonteaching hours affixing words to paper. The result: 30 books, 200 journal articles, 50 research reports, and 175 papers presented before research societies. Although not noted in his official vita, while at UCLA he also authored 1,426 grocery lists.

Dr. Popham's most recent books are *Classroom Assessment: What Teachers Need to Know* (5th ed., 2008) and *Assessment for Educational Leaders* (2006); *The Truth about Testing: An Educator's Call to Action* (2001) and *Test Better, Teach Better: The Instructional Role of Assessment* (2003); *America's "Failing" Schools: How Parents and Teachers Can Cope with No Child Left Behind* (2005) and *Mastering Assessment: A Self-Service System for Educators* (2006). He encourages purchase of these books because he regards receiving their semiannual royalties as psychologically reassuring.

In 1978, Dr. Popham was elected to the presidency of the American Educational Research Association (AERA). He was also the founding editor of *Educational Evaluation and Policy Analysis,* a quarterly journal published by AERA. He has attended each year's AERA meeting since his first in 1958. He is inordinately compulsive.

In 1968, Dr. Popham established the Institutional Objectives Exchange, which then was known as IOX Assessment Associates, an R&D group that formerly created statewide student achievement tests for a dozen states. He has personally passed all of those tests, largely because of his unlimited access to the tests' answer keys.

In 2002, the National Council on Measurement in Education presented Dr. Popham with its Award for Career Contributions to Educational Measurement. In 2006 he was awarded a Certificate of Recognition by the National Association of Test Directors. His complete forty-two-page, single-spaced vita can be requested. It is really dull reading.

Index